DRIVING T
HIGHV
AND CENTRAL AMERICA

A COMPLETE GUIDEBOOK FOR DO-IT-YOURSELF PLANNING, PREPARING FOR, AND DRIVING THROUGH MEXICO AND CENTRAL AMERICA

Written By

RAYMOND & AUDREY PRITCHARD

ALL RIGHTS RESERVED - TODOS DERECHOS RESERVADOS

DRIVING THE PAN-AMERICAN HIGHWAY TO MEXICO AND CENTRAL AMERICA

By Raymond and Audrey Pritchard

Maps, Photos, Update and Spanish Translations: Chris Howard
Photos taken with a Pentax IQZoom 160 camera.

Sixth Edition

First four editions published in Costa Rica

© 1997-8 Costa Rica Books and Raymond Pritchard

ISBN 1-881233-48-0

Costa Rica Books
Suite 1 SJ0 981
P.O. Box 025216
Miami, FL 33102-5216
Tel: 800 365-2342 Fax: 011-506-232-5613
http://www.bookzone.com/costarica

ALL RIGHTS RESERVED. No part of this book may be reproduced without written permission of the authors and copyright owner.

TODOS DERECHOS RESERVADOS. Esta publicación está protegida por las disposiciones legales de impresión y derechos de autor. Queda prohibido cualquier tipo de reproducción, grabación o fotocopiado sin permiso escrito de los autores.

TABLE OF CONTENTS

CHAPTER III

CHAPTER IV

CHAPTER V

CHAPTER VI

ABOUT THE AUTHORS

The author Raymond Pritchard, a former New York travel tour operator and reporter during World War II, couldn't find any books on this subject in libraries or bookstores. So he wrote one. He and his wife Audrey, a one-time airline stewardess with TACA and American Airlines flying into Mexico and Central America, share their experiences in planning and making this adventure-filled journey.

Christopher Howard, the author of the best-selling guide—*The Golden Door to Retirement, Living and Investing in Costa Rica*—and publisher of Mr. Pritchard's guide, updated this edition and supplied the Spanish translations and maps.

FOREWORD

The purpose of this guidebook is to assist those wishing to drive through Mexico and into Central America. The United States was a sleeping giant in the 19th century. The railroads that were built across the country were instrumental in its development. Mexico and Central America are being awakened from their slumber by the building of the Pan-American Highway.

In the future travel, ecotourism and trade agreements will stride hand in hand with industry to create exciting and explosive new growth in this part of the world. This will lead to the development of new tourist meccas for vacationing North Americans and others. Furthermore, the present economy is forcing many retirees and senior citizens, who live on fixed incomes, to seek more affordable housing and life-styles south of the border. Just like the birds facing the coming winter, they will turn to the South in ever greater numbers.

The massive numbers of automobiles in Mexico and the Central American countries assures proper road maintenance and an abundance of modern service stations. Many of these new stations are being equipped with stateside Circle K-type mini-marts and provide complete car care.

The past history of the ancient Aztec and Mayan civilizations are here for us to rediscover. However, the greatest discovery we have in store, are the lovely and fascinating peoples of these countries.

With these things in mind, we have created this annual guidebook as an aid, so you can step out without fear, and enjoy the beauty of this historical part of our hemisphere.

Good news for those of you planning to travel through Central America in the future. On February 2, 1997 the presidents of all the Cenral American countries proposed a joint project to improve the Pan-American Highway. The project will be be financed by the Interamerican Development Bank and backed by the Spanish government. It will include widening, expanding, repairing and reconstructing most of the actual highway as well as some possible route changes. After all of these improvements have been made, one private company will then be put in charge of maintaining the highway in good shape in all of the Central American countries. This will improve the infrastructure of the region, speed up commerce and make travel easier.

DISCLAIMER

We update this annual guidebook in order to make sure the information it contains is as accurate and up to date as possible. It is designed to assist the reader in preparing for and driving the routes covered. The information and advice we provide will facilitate travel through Mexico and Central America. However, we cannot possibly cover every sitution the reader might encounter along the way. This guide is sold with the understanding that the authors and publisher cannot be responsible for any changes in laws, hotel ratings, conditions or prices as stated in this book. It is strongly recommended that the reader contact hotels and consulates before travelling to see if there have been any significant changes in the data we have provided in this guide.

REQUEST FOR INFORMATION

To keep the information as up-to-date as possible for forthcoming editions, please fill out the questionnaire at the end of this guidebook, and return it as requested. We plan to update this guidebook annually, and will give you recognition for your assistance in this endeavor.

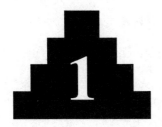

CHAPTER I

PREPARATION FOR THE TRIP

When my wife and I decided we were going to drive to Costa Rica, we had to do a lot of research on the subject. We knew absolutely nothing about the roads and very little about the countries through which we would be driving. When we mentioned the subject to our friends or relatives, we received a lot of negative horror stories that we would be captured and killed by *bandidos* —or at the very least, robbed and raped. Their knowledge came from the ghastly things we have all seen in old Western movies with John Wayne and Clint Eastwood and stories of Mexican bandits like Pancho Villa.

There were times when I was almost convinced I had lost my marbles, or at least was not playing with a full deck for even thinking of such adventure. After all, I was 73 years old with an aorta heart valve that had been replaced with a calf's valve and which was starting to leak again, and here I was looking at driving over 4,000 miles in as short a period of time as possible.

We had very limited funds, and could ill-afford a lot of expensive hotels. The fewer nights we spent en route the better off we would be, financially. We had a seven year old, high mileage, four cylinder mini-van that we were planning to drive. It would take a lot of preparation.

RESEARCHING THE TRIP

The first thing we did was to go to the Automobile Club of Southern California (AAA), where we had been faithful members for many years. We knew they had maps, and we understood they would work up a route analysis for us as part of our membership. When we got there we found that they had excellent maps of California, Arizona, New Mexico, Texas, and even of Mexico. They also had a detailed guidebook of Mexico. To our disappointment, they did not make route surveys for trips outside of the United States, nor did they have maps or any information on Central America. We took the five maps and the Mexico guidebook.

Next, we went to the local library and couldn't find anything about driving to Central America via the Pan-American or any other highway.

We also searched through B. Dalton and a couple of other book stores. There were books about the Aztec and Mayan Civilizations, about the flora and the fauna of all these countries, and about the Spanish conquests of the area, but nothing on how to drive there.

Someone gave me a map supplement to the National Geographic from April, 1986, covering Central America. It picked up where the AAA map of Mexico left off. It was not really a road map, although it did show roads and the various cities, as well as being an excellent topographical map. By using it and a lot of imagination, I was able to highlight the routing that seemed the best. I measured the distances as accurately as possible, then as there would be a lot of mountain driving, I added fifteen percent to the direct distances to make up for the curves and cut-backs. I found that my distances were fairly correct.

As we drove through Guatemala, El Salvador, Honduras, Nicaragua and into Costa Rica, we found there were many Texaco, Shell, Mobile and Chevron stations where you can pick up maps of those countries. You might check with those stations in the U.S., or write to their public relations departments for additional information on where to obtain the maps in the U.S. Also see the excellent detailed maps we advertise on the opposite page. We didn't discovered them until after making our trip through Mexico and Central America.

As I have a son living in Killeen, Texas, we decided to drive via Arizona, New Mexico and Texas, and throw in a little farewell visiting

Detailed Maps
For Your Trip

- Mexico Travel Reference Map
  Scale 1:3,000,000 ....$12.95
- Central American Travel Reference Map
  Scale 1:1,800,000 ....$12.95
- Costa Rica Travel Reference Map $12.95
  Scale 1:500,000
- Guatemala and El Salvador Travel Reference
  Map $12.95
- The Essential Road Guide to Costa Rica (Book) $19.95
    This one-of-a-kind guide contains the maps and routes
  most traveled by tourists and residents. A complete list-
  ing of buses operating in San José, with diagrams of the
  most important San José routes, as well as those from San
  José to all parts of the country.

"If you're going to travel by car or bus, you need this book."

Add $3.00 Postage & Handling to U.S.,
$4.00 to Canada and Latin America
and $5.00 to Europe.
Also add $1.00 for each additional map or product.

Send To:
Costa Rica Books
Suite1 SJO 981• P.O. Box 025216• Miami, FL 33102-5216
http://www.bookzone.com/costarica

Credit Cards
1-800-365-2342

Other Publications
by
Costa Rica Books

- The Golden Door to Retirement and
  Living in Costa Rica $16.95
- Driving the Pan-American Highway to Mexico
  and Central America $18.95
- Buying Real Estate in Costa Rica $24.95
- The Legal Guide to Costa Rica $24.95
- Costa Rican Spanish Survival Booklet
  & 90-Minute Cassette $13.95
- Tico Times Annual Visitors Guide $13.95
- Belize Retirement Guide $19.95
- Happy Aging With Costa Rican Women $19.95
- The Costa Rica Road Guide $19.95
- The Costa Rican Outlook Newsletter ..... $25.00 annually

Videos

- Retire In Costa Rica........ *a tropical paradise*
  (60 minutes) $22.95
- Costa Rica UNICA! $22.95

Send To:

Costa Rica Books

Suite 1 SJO 981 • P.O. Box 025216 • Miami, FL 33102

http://www.bookzone.com/costarica

Credit Cards

1-800-365-2342

Add $3.00 Postage & Handling to U.S.,
$4.00 to Canada and Latin America
and $5.00 to Europe.
Also add $1.00 for each additional book or video.

on the way. In addition, I was afraid the heat at that near sea level of the West Coast route might be too taxing for me. I noticed that the route out of Laredo, Texas followed a much higher elevation and would probably be cooler. Also, there were more industrial cities on that route, which would probably mean more traffic, possibly adding to "safety in numbers" if any of that *"bandido"* talk were true. For these reasons, we decided on the Laredo, Monterrey, Mexico City, Oaxaca routing. However, the East Coast route via Brownsville, Tampico and Veracruz to Guatemala is shorter and considered the best route when driving to Central America.

PICKING YOUR DESTINATION

Now that we had made the decision on the routing, there were many items we needed to research. The reason for writing this guide-book is to, perhaps, fill the void that we had encountered, and to assist others, such as yourselves, in planning your drive south, for whatever reason and destination you may have.

Our reason was that the doctors had told me I must go into full retirement—which we could not afford in California. We would be living on a fixed income of less than $800.00 per month, so we had to plan accordingly.

In our research we found a very low air fare to Costa Rica during the month of October, so we flew there to verify if we could really get by on my monthly Social Security check. In a few years, my wife, Audrey, would be able to add her Social Security to mine to make it a bit easier. So, we had something to look forward to.

We found a lovely home in the mountains above San José, Costa Rica. The owner would hold it for three months on a proposed 5-year lease—so that matter was happily settled.

The next item on our agenda was to get information about moving to Cost Rica. We had been warned that Costa Rican attorneys were the transplanted *"bandidos"* of Mexico. We did not have any idea where to look for a good one. We picked up the local *Tico Times* English lan-guage newspaper, and found that there was a seminar for newcomers that would give us the information we would need to make a decision on whether it would be practical to move or not. At the seminar we found a seemingly very good attorney at an acceptable price, who would get us our *"Pensionado"* papers, and would clear our car and furniture through customs. We also found out what would be required in the way of necessary paperwork to move to Costa Rica or any other country you may select.

We started with our requirements, took our physical for tuberculosis and AIDS, were fingerprinted for Interpol, and got started on our *Pensionado* papers while we were there. The balance of the papers and documents were mailed to our attorney via Federal Express as soon as we returned home.

Now, we figured that our research was over. We had made our decision. The next thing to do was to get the rest of our paperwork together, and get physically ready to move.

REQUIRED DOCUMENTATION

There is a lot of required paperwork that must be completed if you are planning to move, or to just drive into Mexico or Central America. This includes:

1. **PASSPORTS:** You can obtain a "Tourist Card" at the border, through the Mexican Consulate, or through an airline. To continue beyond a certain point in Baja California, or about 25 miles south of the Mexican border or elsewhere into Central America, you will need a passport. You can obtain your passport by making application at many designated post offices. Just phone your nearest post office and they will give you all of the information on the documents you need. When you have the required documents together, take them to the designated post office, pay your fee, and in a few days you will receive your passport by mail. As a suggestion— when you have your passport photos made, you may want to have them take several different shots. Pick out the one that you like best for your passport, and save the others for visas. You never see your visas, but your passport photo is with you for the next ten years.

2. **BIRTH CERTIFICATES:** You must contact the Hall of Records of the county in which you were born to obtain your birth certificate. Once you obtain your certificate, seal it clear plastic covers. *Never* give out your original. Always make photocopies right through the plastic cover, and give them out. Keep the originals in a safe place such as a strong box or safe deposit box.

3. **MARRIAGE LICENSES AND DIVORCE PAPERS:** If you are moving to another country, they will probably want a copy of these documents. This is particularly true in Central and South America, which are predominately Catholic countries. Make photocopies of them and keep your originals with your other documents.

4. **POLICE CLEARANCE:** Most countries require a police clearance. Go to your local police or sheriff's department. Fill out the request forms and pay them a nominal fee. They will mail your clearance in a few days. Keep it with your other documents, and give out photocopies, only. Some countries will require a clearance by Interpol before allowing you in as a resident. This is done by the country to which you are moving.

5. **FINANCIAL RESPONSIBILITY:** Unlike the United States, which seemingly does not require immigrants to be financially sound (in fact it appears that we accept them more readily if we can put them on the welfare rolls immediately), many countries require certain financial guarantees to get into their country as a resident. As an example, to immigrate to Costa Rica to become a *"Pensionado"*, you must have a guaranteed income of $600.00 per month for a couple. A *"Rentista"* must show $1,000.00 per month. A letter signed by an official of the Social Security office will suffice as long as the amount at least equals the requirement. An arrangement can be made between a Costa Rican state bank and your stateside financial institution, where your account is sufficiently sound, for the monthly transfer of at least the minimum required amount. Check with the consulate of the country of your choice to be sure you meet with their financial requirements.

6. **CERTIFICATE OF AUTO INSURANCE:** If you plan to drive more than about twenty-five miles (in most cases) into Mexico, or pass through Mexico on your way to Central America, you must have Mexican Automobile Insurance. Most American insurance policies are void as soon as you cross over the border. (We suggest that you check this out with your insurance agent). We checked the "yellow pages" of the Los Angeles phone directory and found a Mexico Insurance Company with an "800" phone number. We called them, then faxed our U.S. insurance policy (the typed page with all of the details about your car), and authorization to charge it to our credit card. We gave them the dates we planned to be in Mexico (they charge by the day). Within an hour I had a fax copy

of my policy, and the next day I received the actual policy in the mail. Check your yellow pages. Also, you can buy the insurance at the border. There are usually several insurance offices as you approach the border. It is fast. My policy cost $13.00 per day for full coverage.

Californians driving into Mexico will find the red tape easier to negociate thanks to a new agreement that allows an American company to issue tourist permits to American travellers.

The agreement between Mexican Ministries of Tourisim and Sanborn's International Insurance services of McAllen, Texas, permits motorists to fill out immigration and customs forms and have them stamped before they enter Mexico at any of the 23 offices along Mexico's border with California, Arizona, New Mexico and Texas. With the proper documents in hand, a motoring tourist arriving at the border need only to go to the Banjército (Mexican Army Bank) window at Mexican Customs. There, travellers present their documents, pay an adminstrative fee of about $12 and receive a car sticker. The alternative is to do all the paperwork at the border, which means standing in several lines—a process that can take hours at the worst. For a list of Sanborn's locations, contact **Sanborn's Insurance**, 2009 S. 10th St., McAllen, Tex 78503; Tel: (210) 686-0711, Fax: (210) 686-0732 or toll free at 800 222-0158.

Sanborn's provides a booklet full of information and services for a care-free driving trip to Mexico and Central America. Sanborn's is the ONLY company to offer Central American Insurance for both you and your vehicle. They also provide you with a helpful publication called *Travelog* for overland travel all the way to Panama. It guides you mile-by-mile to your destination and back and is a good supplement to this book. For questions about Central American Travel call their resident Central American Expert at (210) 682-1354. You may also join Sanborn's Amigo Club for additonal privileges and travel benefits. Call their 800 number for more details. Another good feature Sanborn's offers is that if you overstay your policy in any of the countries and it expires, you can extend it by just giving them your credit card number by phone or fax.

The **American Auotombile Association (AAA)** offfers insurance and similar services in Arizona, New Mexico and Texas, but not in California. The AAA decided not to become involved in the stamping of documents because many Californians go to Baja California, where they are not required. **Anserv Insurance Services** (tel: 800-2621994)and **International Gateway Insurance Brokers** (tel: 800 -423-2646) are other companies which provide Mexican automobile insurance.

7. **MEXICAN RULES REGARDING ACCIDENTS:** It is important to know and understand that Mexican laws and rules differ from those in the United States. In the U. S. you are considered innocent until proven guilty. In Mexico it is the reverse. You are considered guilty until proven innocent. If you are in an accident where someone is injured or killed, whether it was your fault or not, in all probability, you will go to jail. Contact your Mexican Insurance Company immediately, and have them get an attorney for you. Remember , you are in their country and their laws prevail.

8. **PROOF OF OWNERSHIP OR PERMISSION STATEMENT:** When you cross the border into Mexico, be sure to tell the border guard that you are driving deep into Mexico. Otherwise, he may think you are just going to shop in the border city. If you do not do this, he may wave you through, and a few miles down the road, you will come to a check point. If you do not have the proper sticker on your windshield, and are not properly documented, he will probably send you back to the border to get it. At the office where the sticker is issued, they will make photocopies of your "pink slip" (ownership certificate), passport and drivers license. If you do not have your pink slip because your car is not paid off, you *must* go to the financial institution who holds the pink slip (title) and get an authorization letter stating their approval for you to drive the car into Mexico. Once you have satisfied the officials that the paperwork is correct and it matches the numbers on the car, they will place a sticker on your windshield. As you come to checkpoints in the country, the guards will check your papers against the numbers on your car and your windshield sticker. Guatemala was the only other country we encountered that put a sticker on our car. They were not as thorough as Mexico. I guess they figure that if you got all of the way through Mexico, it must be right.

9. **OBTAINING YOUR 'DRIVE THROUGH' VISAS:** One thing that is very important, and that will save you time and problems at the border crossings, is to obtain your "drive through" visas in advance. Determine your routing, then contact the consulates for each of the countries you will pass through, and arrange for your

visas. The regulation are subject to <u>change</u> from time to time. So, contact your nearest consulate in advance to find out the most recent requirements. We phoned each of the consulates and found out the following:

A. MEXICO: Required our passport and extra passport photos. The charges were $21.00 per person. Call (202) 728-1750 in the U.S. and (604) 669-2845 in Canada.

B BELIZE: If you plan to travel through the Yucatan peninsula to this country, check with your local consulate. You may call the consulate in Washington (202) 332-9636 or Los Angeles at (213) 469-7346.

C. GUATEMALA: Required our passport which they stamped. The charges were $10.00 per person. Call (202) 745-4952 in the U.S. and (613) 237- 3941 in Canada.

D. EL SALVADOR.: Required our passport which they stamped. There was no charge. Call (202) 265-3480 in the U.S. and (613) 238-2939 in Canada.

E. HONDURAS: At present no visa is required. They stamped our passport at the border. Call (202) 966-7700 in the U.S. and (604) 685-7711 in Canada.

F. NICARAGUA: They did not require visas. They stamped our passports at the border. Call (202) 939-6531 in the U.S. and (613) 238-7677 in Canada.

G. COSTA RICA: They did not require visas. They stamped our passports at the border. Call (202) 328-6628 in the U.S. and (604) 682-3865 in Canada.

H. PANAMA: U.S. and Canadians only need a $5 tourist card. Call (202) 387-6145 in the U.S. and (416) 822-0488 in Canada.

NOTE: At this writing, the above countries are negotiating for a "no inspection" system, similar as crossing from one state into another in the U.S. This may or may not be in effect at the time of your planned crossings. We managed to get our visas in two days. If we had found out their hours in advance and planned accordingly, we probably could have done it in one day, as some of the consulates closed at 1:00 p.m.

Now that you have completed your legal requirements, you can really get ready for your trip.

FINANCES FOR THE TRIP

Unfortunately, we let the *"bandido"* factor influence us too much in preparing our financial arrangements. Everyone we talked to suggested we take travellers checks. The idea of having them replaced if they are lost or stolen is great. The problem comes up that about the only place you can cash them is in the four and five star hotels. If there were offices where you could cash them around the service stations and motels, it would be great. If you are trying to "poor boy" it in the $20.00 per night motels instead of the $100.00 luxury hotels, you could have problems if you go heavy on the travellers checks. Compute your costs in advance. Divide your total anticipated mileage by the fuel consumption rate of your car, and multiply that by $1.50 per gallon. That is the approximate amount of cash you will need for fuel for the trip. If you are staying at the Holiday Inns or equivalent, you will have no problem with travellers checks or credit cards. If not, you can plan on stopping in them for breakfast and cashing your daily need of travellers checks.

I suggest that you take quite a bit of cash and divide it up into 3 or 4 bundles and hide it in your car or luggage. Do not carry it all in one place. In spite of what some people say, you will need U.S. cash and local currency at places I have already mentioned, plus each border crossing will take from $20.00 to $50.00 to get through. There are a lot of "hands" out there, as we will discuss later.

PREPARING YOUR CAR FOR THE TRIP

If you are driving a new car, you should't have any problems. Just change your oil and you are nearly ready—except for one important detail. Go to the trunk of your car and look at the spare tire. If it is one of those little "doughnuts", go to an auto wrecker and pick up a full size wheel. Be sure it is the same size as those on your car. Count the number of "lug holes" in your spare, and be sure the wheel you are buying has the same number. Then go to a tire shop and get a good spare tire. Whoever invented those small tires should have four of them on his hearse. They are no earthly good—especially in the middle of the Mexican desert.

If you plan to bring extra tires, it may be advisable to have them mounted on spare wheels. One person that I talked to had four new spare tires that were not mounted. He had no problems until he came to the Department of Health checkpoint at the Costa Rican border. There, they confiscated the tires. There is a law in Costa Rica that all tires must be mounted on a wheel or rim. The reason is that water can collect in the tires, and will become a breeding place for mosquitoes. One man got through who had blown-up tubes in his tires. This man with the four tires was given three days to get the tires mounted on wheels. There was a convenient garage near-by which sold wheels, and that would mount the tires for him. Of course, this would be costly. We may not understand or agree with this law, but in their country, their laws prevail.

Get a grease job on your car. Be sure they check all of the fluid levels and your wheel bearings. Also have them check all of your belts and hoses. Some people suggest that you carry spares—but frankly, I would not know how to replace them if I did have them. Of course, you could always find a mechanic to replace them for you. Modern Mexico and Central America have lots of good service stations and garages to help you. In fact, I have driven in many areas of the United States that are far worse than Mexico and Central America for car service.

A modern gas station and minimarket on the Pan-American Highway.

Replace worn tires, and be sure to check your brake pads. I suggest that you go to the car dealer of your model, or a trustworthy auto parts store, and buy one or two extra sets of good brake pads for your disc brakes. The ones you buy in these countries are of poor quality. I had a new pair of "local" brake pads wear out in a month. You can pay the brake shop to install your new stateside brake pads for you.

One thing that wore out on my trip was my fuel filter. You will know when it is bad. Your car will act like it is out of gas—even though your fuel gauge says otherwise. They are inexpensive, so toss one in your trunk. Even I can change one in about ten minutes. If you vehicle uses unleaded fuel you may have to change the catalytic converter so your car can run on regular. You can modify your car by simply taking off the catalytic converter and replacing it with a straight piece of exhaust pipe. Ask a mechanic about this.

Be sure you have an assortment of tools—vice grips, crescent wrenches (3 sizes), small pry bar, hammer and two screw driver sets one regular and one Phillips, both in large and small sizes, and an Allen wrench set. We have provided you with a list of tools and possible car problems in Spainsh in Chapter 3.

PACKING YOUR CAR FOR THE TRIP

If you are driving to Costa Rica, for instance, you will be driving through five countries and into the sixth. That means eleven border checks. You usually do not have a problem leaving a country—it is entering them where the problems seem to arise. Most of the guards are either underpaid, or they like the authority to be able to harass the "*gringo*". Of course, many are looking for a "pay-off" or bribe for not searching your car. However, an attempted bribe could make you suspect.

There are a couple of things you can do to possibly avoid these car strip-search situations (where they make you completely unload everything from your car). As you pack the bags and boxes that you are taking, affix a number on each of them, and make a list of what is in each piece of luggage, and have it translated into Spanish. Make several photocopies of this list. When you come to a customs check, give them a copy of this list, properly numbered to coincide with the luggage. Do not list the contents on the box, as that could make it too easy for selected theft. This may suffice to prevent a shake-down search. But when they tell you to unload, you are at their mercy. It is best that you cooperate with them.

Remember one thing. You will not be travelling in California where the law requires clean, equipped rest rooms. You will find most restrooms are filthy by our standards—most without seats and no paper. My wife always carries her large straw bag with a roll of toilet paper and a few toilet seat covers folded in it. The newer Pemex (in Mexico) and Shell, Texaco and Unocal stations in Central America are considerably upgraded, but do not depend on it.

One of the most useful items on our trip was a fold-up port-a-potty, which uses throw-away plastic bags. As we drove along, we would find an open stretch of road, and pull off the highway —then head back at a 45-degree angle toward the road. I would stop and open the passenger side front door. This made a secluded area where I placed the port-a-potty. My wife preferred that to possible filthy rest rooms you are faced with as an alternative. After our first "pit stop", we found it best not to use the plastic bags, as they only caused litter and a disposal problem. A little water or fertilizer is good for the desert when properly buried.

BORDER CROSSINGS

Without a doubt the most difficult and annoying part of you trip will be the delays and inconveniences at the Central American border crossings. Be prepared for a lot of headaches. Depending on which route you travel, you will have to cross at least seven borders if you travel throughMexico all the way to Panama. Be prepared to spend at least several frustrating hours at some of the crossings. Then you just clear one border and drive a short distance to the next country, only to have to have to go through the whole dilatory process again. On top of that some of officials seem to always be in a bad mood and there are a lot of other people hitting you up for money. All of this while your papers are being shuttled from office to office as you wonder if everything is all right. Speaking some Spanish will somewhat ease your anxiety.

There is a whole mini-industry to guide travellers through the bureaucratic maze of paperwork at each border. Young men and teenage boys will eagerly help you process your papers. You don't have to look for them. They will bombard you as soon as you reach the border. You will have to give them a tip of a couple of dollars. This really makes this process a lot easier and saves you a lot of footwork. They will guide you through the whole process. These people are especially helpful if you don't speak Spanish. Carry some U.S. dollars in small denominations to tip these young helpers and pay your fees. You can usually get away with paying no more than $25 - $30 at each border including tips. When you pull up to a border don't make the mistake of getting in the same lane as large trucks. Go to the car lane. If you go to the end of the truck line, it will take much longer to get through customs.

One long-time resident of Costa Rica told us that after making the trip eight time, he finally discovered the secret to getting through the borders quickly. On his last trip he brought a fierce looking German shephard with him in his car. Nobody got near his car to inspect it and he was ushered through most border crossing quickly. If you plan to use this strategy, check each country's health requiements for your pet.

Here is a list of all the border and more less what to expect:

MEXICO: Probably the easiest of the borders to cross since there is so much traffic between the U.S. and Mexico. Most major crossings ar opened 24-hours. Customs officials are use to dealing with travellers and have streamlined the whole process. No bribes, no extra fees and no waiting. Your papers will be processed quickly provided all of your papers are in order (check all of the requirements in Chapter 3). You will need a passport, birth certificate, tourist card, vehicle registration (if you don't own the car a notarized letter form the owner), and a valid driver's license. If you are traveling longer than 72 hours in Mexico you will need to get two important documents from Mexican customs: *Solicitud de Importación Temporal* or temporary vehicle importation permit, and a *Promesa de Retornar El Vehículo* or promisary note to return your car when leaving the country from Mexican customs. Once again, Sanborn's Insurance will take care of all of this for you, if you stop by one of their many locations.

When all of your paper work is approved you then have to go to a *Banjército* (military Bank) office next to the custom's building. You credit card will be charged $12 for a permit fee(There is a copy of Banjército forms and booklet in Chapter 3). You have to pay by credit card. If you don't have a credit card you will have to pay a bond which can be expensive for newer model cars. Once this is done you are issued a sticker that is attached to your front windshield. When you exit Mexico you will have to turn in your vehicle permit. Always have your car permit with you since there are secondary checkpoints along the route. A word of warning: If you keep your car in Mexico for longer than the law permits, you may be fined. You won't have to worry about this if you are just travelling through the county.

BELIZE: You enter via Chemul, Mexico. You have to provide proof of liability insurance in order to get your car into the country. You exit the country at the town of Benque Viejo del Carmen. This border crossing is supposedly open 24 hours a day but usualy closes between midnight and 6a.m.

GUATEMALA: The best place to cross the border is at the town of Tecún Umanán across the border form Tapachula, Mexico. Spend the night in Tapachula so you can get an eary start in the morning. This way you should be able to cross the country in one day. However, just south of Tapachula the highway divides between the mountain and coastal routes before entering Guatemala. It is faster to take the coastal route and bypass Guatemala City if you are in a hurry. Much as we descibed at the beginning of this section there will be a long line of cars trucks and buses waiting to enter the country. You will be beseiged with people trying to help move your paperwork through the laberynth of customs. You will also have to have your car fumigated.

EL SALVADOR: You have two choices when leaving Gualtemala, to go through Honduras or via El Salavador and a little piece of western Honduras which is the shortest and quickest way. You need to show all of your papers including your driver's license and proof of ownership. The procedure and ordeal is much like the rest of the border crossings we have desceibed.

HONDURAS: The main border crossing to Honduras is at El Amàtillo. If you start early from almost any place in El Salvador you can cross the short stretch of Honduras in a couple of hours and make it to one of Nicaragua's main cities the same day. The Honduran border is renowned for being the worst in Central America. It will usually cost you the most money. You will have to pay off a lot of officials to process your vehicle. Use a runner as at the other borders. In theory the borders are opened daily from around 7am to 5 pm. Be aware that you may be stopped several times and asked for your papers while driving through the coutry. You may have to pay a couple of small bribes to avoid hastles at checkpoints.

NICARAGUA: Nicaragua has three overland border crossings from Honduras. The most inland one is at is at at Las Manos near Ocotal which you will probably take if you are com ing from Tegucigalpa; the second is at El Espino near Somoto on Central American Highway 1 or CA-1. The fastest route form Cholteca, Honduras to Nicaragua is at Guasaule between El Triunfo (Honduras) and Somotillo (Nicaragua).

From there you head toward León, Nicaragua and if all goes well you will be in Costa Rica in a matter of hours.

COSTA RICA: After Mexico, Costa Rica has by far the smoothest border operation. The border is a breeze compared to the other Central American countries. The border crossing is located at the town of Peñas Blancas. Customs are opened on the Costa Rican side from 8 am to 5 pm daily and until 4 pm on the Nicraguan side. It is about one mile between the Costa Rican and Nicaraguan immigration offices. If you plan to go on to Panama, you will exit Costa Rica at Paso Canoas on the Pan-American Highway or CA-1.

PANAMA: This is a busy border because of the large amount of commerical traffic between Costa Rica and Panama. The border crossing at Paso Canoas is open from 7 am to 10 pm on the Costa Rica side and 24 hours on the Panamanian side. Panamanian customs also run smoothly. There is a time change in Panama, so don't forget to change your watch.

ADDITIONAL TIPS

1) Watch for speed traps in Honduras, Costa Rica and Panama. Above all, if you do get a ticket, be courteous.

2) Do not make this trip alone. We know a couple of Americans who have done it, but there can be problems.

3) Budget your time and money accordingly.

4) Travel with original documents and have any important papers translated into Spanish.

5) Be sure not to leave any valuables in your car when it is unattended.

6) Again, make sure you car is good mechanical shape.

7) Keep your cash, traveller's checks and other small valuables in a money belt.

8) Have a lot of dollar bills to hand out for tips.

9) Get all of your tourist visas ahead of time.

10) Find out all of the current exchange rates before you reach the border, so you won't get ripped off.

11) When travelling hide your money in several places in the car so as to not have all of it in one place.

12) Don't carry handguns unless you like to spend time in jail and pay huge fines.

13) Make sure you understand the right-of-way system for each country.

14) Don't go off onto any side roads or unmarked routes.
15) NEVER drive at night.

READY...SET...GO !

So now you have completed your paperwork, selected your routing, checked and loaded your car, studied our tips and advice, you are ready to begin your exciting journey.

The next chapter outlines several suggested routes, with a break down of possible stop-over cities, times and mileages.

Just so you can see how such our trip to Costa Rica transpired , we have outlined our day by day encounters and observations along our route from Laredo, Texas to San José, Costa Rica in Chapter 4. This will give you an idea of what to expect. We hope it will be of help to you.

We have also contacted a number of people who have made this trip. This includes those who have travelled by RV—either by themselves or in a caravan, and even one family who drove down pulling a 4,000 pound trailer. Many were nice enought to provide us with detailed accounts of their trips in Chapter 5.

By the way, if you are planning to travel through Mexico with a RV, trailer or camper, we suggest you read, *RV Travels in Mexico* by John Howells (see the back of this book for details). This great guide contains an extensive list of trailer parks throughout Mexico. It has many valuable suggestions to help you travel in safety and comfort plus much more.

While on your trip, please make notes of such things as road conditions; hotel, motel and trailer park costs; other accommodations; interesting encounters; costs at border crossings and anything else of interest to others. Your information may be used in future guidebooks. You will be given special mention if we decide to use your material. Thank you.

CHAPTER II

RECOMMENDED ROUTES

On the following pages you will find route maps of Mexico and Central America. For Mexico we have indicated four points of entry from the United States. These include:

(1) **NOGALES.** This routing takes you along the West Coast of the Mexico mainland through Hermosillo, Guaymas, Mazatlán, Puerto Vallarta and Acapulco, where you join the inland routes at Tehuantepec. You may also leave the coastal route at Tepic and go through Guadalajara to Mexico City and south to the border.

(2) **EL PASO.** This routing takes you via Durango to San Luis Potosí, where you will join the central route south.

(3) **LAREDO.** This routing takes you via Monterrey to San Luis Potosí— where you join the central route south.

(4) **BROWNSVILLE.** You may join the central route at San Luis Potosí, or may continue along the Gulf Coast through Tampico and Veracruz to the Yucatan Peninsula and Belize. You also have the option of cutting across the isthmus at Acayucan and joining the central route near Tehuantepec and then to the Guatemalan border

RECOMMENDED ROUTES - MEXICO

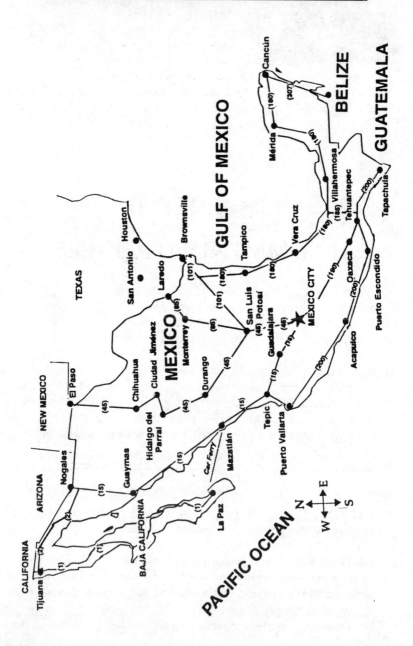

RECOMMENDED ROUTES - CENTRAL AMERICA

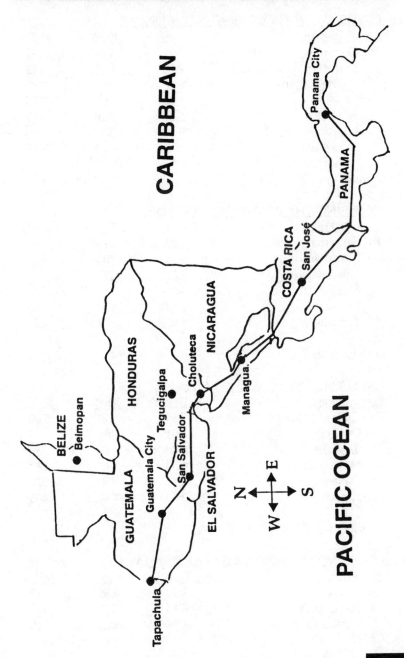

ROUTES, TIMES AND DISTANCES FOR MEXICO AND CENTRAL AMERICA

1. CROSSING THE BORDER AT NOGALES, AZ

From Nogales	Time	Km*	Miles
To: Guaymas	5:23	419	252
Mazatlán	9:12	803	482
Puerta Vallarta	6:45	462	277
La Mira	8:36	361	217
Acapulco	5:26	361	217
Puerto Escondido	5:50	339	204
Tapachula	9:49	692	415

Go to route map 7

2. CROSSING THE BORDER AT NOGALES, AZ

From Nogales	Time	Km*	Miles
To: Guaymas	5:23	419	252
Mazatlán	9:12	803	482
Guadalajara	7:57	521	313
Mexico City+	9:19	563	338
Oaxaca	7:41	450	270
Tapachula	9:05	674	405

Go to route map 7

3. CROSSING THE BORDER AT EL PASO, TX

From El Paso	Time	Km*	Miles
To: Ciudad Jimenez	7:54	600	360
Durango	6:51	488	293
San Luis Potosí	6:40	481	289
Mexico City+	4:58	413	248
Oaxaca	7:41	450	270
Tapachula	9:05	674	405

Go to route map 7

4. CROSSING THE BORDER AT LAREDO, TX

From Laredo	Time	Km*	Miles
To: Monterrey	3:20	236	142
San Luis Potosí	6:18	537	322
Mexico City+	4:58	413	248

Oaxaca	7:41	450	270
Tapachula	9:05	674	405

Go to route map 7

5. CROSSING BORDER AT BROWNSVILLE, TX

From Brownsville	Time	Km*	Miles
To: San Luis Potosí	9:09	720	423
Mexico City+	4:58	413	248
Oaxaca	7:41	450	270
Tapachula	9:05	674	405

Go to route map 7

6. CROSSING BORDER AT BROWNSVILLE, TX

From Brownsville	Time	Km*	Miles
To: Tampico	7:06	504	303
Veracruz	8:05	502	302
Villahermosa	8:39	530	318
Mérida	8:39	621	385
Cancún	4:23	319	192
Belize	8:10	583	350

7 FROM TAPACHULA, MEXICO TO PANAMA CITY

From Tapachula	Time	Km*	Miles
To: Guatamala City	4:30	294	176
San Salvador	2:00	183	110
Choluteca	2:40	285	135
Managua	2:18	212	127
San Jose	5:15	423	253
Panama City	8:36	701	419

Km* = Kilometer(s)
+ = Alternate for Mexico City = Puebla or Cuernavaca

It is strongly recommended that you plan each day's drive so you will reach your destination before dark.

Cities selected are suggestions, only. It is possible to combine two or more cities into one day's drive, however you should allow two hours for each border crossing.

CHAPTER III

YOUR TRIP - COUNTRY
BY COUNTRY

When we left California for Costa Rica by car, we knew very little about the countries through which we would be driving. Our goal was to get to Costa Rica as quickly as possible. My wife, Audrey, was a stewardess for T.A.C.A. Airlines some years ago, which flew to all of the capital cities of Central America. For her training, the airline gave her a comprehensive tour of Guatemala. Later with American Airlines, she was assigned to the Mexico City run, and spent a lot of time in Mexico City and Cuernavaca. She knew quite a bit about both Mexico City and Cuernavaca, as well as Chichicastenago, Guatemala. We did have a quick look at the Mexico City/Cuernavaca area on our trip, but did not have the time to see any of the sights of Guatemala.

The purpose of this chapter is to acquaint you, first, with the road signs and a bit of the language that may assist you in your task of driving. Hopefully, it will also highlight some of the important features of each country you will pass through, and trigger your desire to visit some of them. After all, there is an abundance of fascinating places to see, since the Aztec and Mayan civilizations reached such advanced levels in their culture, architecture and works of art.

By studying this area ourselves, and with the help of the Tourist Department of each country, we have made a brief outline of some of the attractions you may wish to visit along the way. We hope this will open the door for some wonderful new experiences and help you with your adventure south of the border

We are presenting the countries in the order that we passed through them, from the United States through Mexico, Guatemala, El Salvador, Honduras, Nicaragua, Costa Rica and Panama. Belize, also a part of Central America, can be included for those wanting to travel via the Yucatan Peninsula through Belize, then to Guatemala, where you can pick up our trip at Guatemala City.

Our presentations are necessarily brief. For more in-depth descriptions of the most important sights in each country, we suggest that you check with your bookstore, library or the Tourist Bureau of the country of interest. There are two books which cover all of the countries exceptionally well: Lonely Planet's *Central America On A Shoestring*, and Passport Book's, Annual *Mexico & Central American Handbook*. Both guides are packed with useful information and provide detailed descriptions of every Central American country. We have also listed more books in the section titled, "Suggested Reading" at the end of this guide.

For Mexico, as there are several possible routes for you to choose from, we have listed the routes from west to east, and have not duplicated the description of any cities that are included on more than one route. Please see the route map of Mexico we have provided in this guidebook.

Thank you.

The Authors

HIGHWAY SIGNS

LOAD LIMIT

NO PEDESTRIANS

PARKING LIMIT

ONE-HOUR PARKING

NO LEFT TURN

NO U TURN

NO PARKING

KEEP RIGHT

INSPECTION

NO TRUCKS

PEDESTRIANS
FACE TRAFFIC

SPEED LIMIT
(IN K.P.H.)

CONTINUOUS TURN

NO BICYCLES

NO PASSING

HORIZONTAL
CLEARANCE

USE RIGHT LANE

DO NOT ENTER

HIGHWAY SIGNS

SLIPPERY ROAD
LOOSE GRAVEL

STEEP HILL

YIELD
RIGHT-OF-WAY

STOP

LANDSLIDE AREA

BUMPS

NARROW BRIDGE

DIP

TWO-WAY TRAFFIC

TRAFFIC CIRCLE

SIGNAL

R.R. CROSSING

CATTLE

SCHOOL CROSSING

MEN WORKING

VERTICAL
CLEARANCE

TRAILER CAMP

AIRPORT

HOSPITAL

MECHANIC

FERRY

RESTAURANT

REST ROOMS

TELEPHONE

GAS STATION

HIGHWAY SIGNS AND DIRECTIONS

Abierto	Open
Aduana	Customs
ALTO.	Stop
Arena Suelta	Loose gravel or sand
Autopista...	Tollroad or Freeway
Bajada	Downgrade
Báscula	Scale
Camino Angosto	Narrow Road
Camino En Reparación	Road Under Repair
Camino Resbaloso	Slippery Road
Camino Sinuoso	Winding Road
Carros Entrando	Merging Traffic
Ceda El Paso	Yeild the Right-of-way
Cerrado	Closed
Circulación	Traffic
Conserve Su Derecho	Keep Right
Cruce de Caminos	Cross Road
Cuidado Con El Ganado	Watch out for Cattle
Cuidado con El Tren	Watch out for Train
Cuota	Toll Road
Curva	Curve
Curva Doble	Double Curve
Curva Peligrosa	Dangerous Curve
Depresión	Dip
Derrumbe	Slide Area
Despacio	Slow
Desviación	Detour
Doble Circulación, Doble Vía	Two-Way Traffic
Enpalme	Junction
Entrada	Driveway, Entrance
Escuela	School
Estacionamiento, Parqueo	Parking Lot
Frene Con El Motor	Brake with the Motor
Fin Del Pavimiento	End of Pavement
Grava Suelta	Loose Gravel
Hombres Trabajando	Men Working
Libre	Free, No Toll
Límite	Limit
Maneje Con Cuidado	Drive Carefully
Máquinas Trabajando	Heavy Equipment Working
No Hay Paso	Road Closed

No Vire a La Derecha .... No Right Turn
No Vire a La Izquierda .... No Left Turn
Parada .... Bus Stop
Parada Obligatoria .... Full Stop
Peatones .... Pedestrians
Peligro .... Danger
Poblado Próximo .... Approaching Town
Precaución .... Caution
Preferencia .... Right-of-Way, Through Traffic
Prohibida Vuelta a La Derecha .... No Right Turn
Prohibida Vuelta a La Izquierda .... No Left Turn
Puente Provisional .... Temporary Bridge
Reduzca, Modere Su Velocidad .... Slow Down
Revisión Fiscal .... Customs Inspection
Salida .... Exit
Se Prohibe Estacionar .... No Parking
Subida .... Steep Up-grade
Topes, Vibradores, Reductor de Velocidad .... Speed Bumps
Tramo En Reparación .... Road Repairs
Tránsito .... Traffic
Un Solo Carril .... One Lane
Vado .... Dip
Velocidad Máxima .... Maximum Speed

CAR PARTS

El Acelarador .... Accelerator
El Alternador .... Alternator
El Arranque .... Starter
La Batería .... Battery
El Baúl, Cajuela .... Trunk
La Bobina .... Coil
La Bocina, Klaxon .... Horn
La Bomba de Agua .... Water Pump
La Bomba de Gasolina .... Fuel Pump
Las Bujías, Candelas .... Spark Plugs
La Cámara, El Tubo .... Tire Tube
El Cambio de Velocidad .... Gear Shift
El Capo .... Hood
El Carburador .... Carburator
La Correa, Banda de Ventilador .... Fan Belt
El Distribuidor .... Distributor
El Eje .... Axle

El Embraque, Clutch .... Clutch
El Encendido.. Ignition
El Escape .... Exhaust System
El Faro Delantero .... Headlight
El Faro Trasero.. Tail Light
El Filtro de Aceite .... Oil Filter
El Freno de Emergencia .... Emergency Brake
Los Frenos.. Brakes
El Generador .... Generator
La Grúa.. Tow Truck
El Guardabarros .... Fender
El Indicador de Dirección, Direccionales .... Turn Signal
La Llanta... Tire
El Limpiaparabrisas.. Windshield Wiper
El Líquido de Frenos .... Brake Fluid
El Parachoques .... Bumper
El Pedal de Clutch .... Clutch Pedal
Piezas, Repuestos, Refracciones............................... Car Parts
El Radiador .... Radiator
El Radio .... Radio
La Refraccionería, Asesorios Automotrices .... Auto Parts Store
El Refrigerante..Coolant
El Regulador de Voltaje .... Voltage Regulator
El Silenciador .... Muffler
El Sistema Eléctrico .... Electrical System
El Tanque .... Gas Tank
El Tapón de Gasolina ....Gas Cap
El Termóstato .... Thermostat
El Tirador de Puerta .... Door handle
La Transmisión .... Transmission
Las Válvulas .... Valves
El Ventilador.. Fan
El Volante .... Steering Wheel

TOOLS, ETC.

El Alambre .... Wire
Los Alicates, Las Pinzas ....Pliers
La Bombilla .... Bulb
La Cinta .... Tape
El Clavo .... Nail
El Desarmador de Cruz .... Phillips Screwdriver
El Destonillador... Screwdriver

El Embudo	Funnel
La Ferretería	Hardware Store
El Gato	Jack
Las Herramientas	Tools
La Llave de Bujías	Spark Plug Wrench
La Llave de Cruz	Lugwrench
La Llave de Torque	Torque Wrench
La Llave Española	Open End Wrench
La Llave Inglesa	Monkey Wrench
La Literna, El Foco	Flashlight
Las Luces Bengalas	Flares
El Malacate	Winch
El Matillo	Hammer
La Matraca	Ratchet
El Papel de Lija	Sandpaper
El Perico	Crescent Wrench
El Perno	Bolt
Las Pinzas de Presión	Vice Grip Pliers
Los Platinos	Points
El Rotor	Rotor
El Soldador	Soldering Iron
Las Tijeras	Scissors
El Tornillo	Screw, Vise
La Tuerca	Nut

CAR TROUBLE

Mi coche está descompuesto, se ha averiado	My car has broken down.
No tengo gasolina	I'm out of gas
Necesito un mecánico	I need a mechanic.
Necesito una grúa, un remolque	I need a tow.
Mi motor se está sobrecalentando	My engine is overheating.
No arranca	It won't start.
Necesito un empujón	I need a push.
¿Hay un taller por aquí?	Is there a repair shop near here ?
¿Hay una gasolinera por aquí?	Is there a gas station near here?
Las llaves están encerradas adentro del coche .	The keys are locked inside.
La batería está muerta, descargada	The battery is dead.
No funciona	Doesn't work.
El radiador tiene un agujero, hueco	The radiator has a leak.
Se pinchó una llanta	I have a flat tire.
Ayúdeme a empuJar mi coche	Help me push my car.
¿Puede arreglar mi llanta?	Can you fix my tire?

Ayúdeme a cambiar la llanta. .... Help me change the tire.
Llene el tanque de gasolina, el radiador de agua ...... Fill the tank with gas,
                                              the radiator with water.
¿Tiene gasolina sin plomo? .... Do you have un-leaded gas ?
Hay un cortocircuito .... There is a short circuit.
La dirección está descompuesta .... The steering doesn't work.
Cambie la manguera del radiador .... Change the radiator hose.
Cambie el aceite .... Change the oil.
Cambie las bujías ....Change the spark plugs.
El tubo de gasolina está tapado ....The gas line is clogged.
Hay un cortocircuito .... There is a short circuit.
Cambie la llanta .... Change the tire.
La llanta de repuesto, refracción ....Spare tire
Ponga agua en la batería .... Put water in the battery.
Favor de afinar el motor .... Please tune the motor.
Láveme el coche .... Wash my car.
Favor de lubricar el coche. .... Lubricate the car.
Por favor, revise .... Please check
El motor suena .... The motor makes sounds.
Favor de ajustar los frenos .... Please adjust the brakes.
Favor de ajustar el clutch .... Please adjust the clutch.
Favor de purgar los frenos ....Please bleed the brakes.
Mi carro está atascado en lodo .... My car is stuck in the mud.
Doble tracción .... Four wheel drive.
¿Dónde está el teléfono público más cercano? .... Where is the nearest
                                              pay phone ?

BORDER CROSSINGS

Los papeles, los documentos .... Papers, documents
Tarjeta de turista .... Tourist Card
La visa .... Visa
El pasaporte .... Passport
El título de propiedad .... Title, ownership papers
¿Tiene algo que declarar? .... Do you have anything to declare ?
No tengo nada que declarar ....I have nothing to declare.
¡Baje las maletas, equipaje! .... Take out your bags!
Abra las maletas ....Open your suitcases.
Hacer contrabando .... To smuggle
Contrabandista .... Smuggler
Sello .... Passport stamp
Nacionalidad .... Nationality
Mi llamo es .... My name is
Viaje de negocios .... Business trip

Viaje de placer .... Pleasure trip, vacation
Estoy de vacaciones .... On vacation.
Soltero .... Single
Casado .... Married
Viudo/a .... Widower/Widow
Seguros .... Insurance
Son regalos .... They are gifts.
Fecha de nacimiento .... Date of birth.
Profesión .... Profession, Job
Dirección .... Address
Viajo a .... I'm traveling to.
Destino final .... Final destination
¿Cuánto tardarán los tramites? .... How long will the paperwork take?
Tengo prisa .... I'm in a hurry.
¿Cuánto le debo? .... How much do I owe you?
Artículos usados .... Used items
Licencia de conductor .... Driver's license
La aduana .... Customhouse
Fianza .... Bond
Un permiso .... Permit
El número de la placa .... License plate number
Revisar, inspeccionar .... To inspect
¿Cuál es el tipo de cambio? .... What is the rate of exchange?
Número de cilindros .... Number of cilinders
Número de puertas .... Number of doors
Número de motor .... Motor number
Año del Vehículo .... Year of car

POLICE

Multa, infracción .... Ticket
¿Qué he hecho? .... What have I done?
No he hecho nada malo .... I haven't done anything wrong.
Estoy perdido .... I'm lost.
¿Cómo se llega a? .... How do I get to?
Me puede indicar el camino .... Can you show me the way?
No conozco los reglamentos de su país .... I am not familiar with your
country's traffic rules.
Ha excedido la velocidad máxima .... You were speeding.
Ceder el paso, dar campo .... Yield the right-of-way.
Advertencia .... Warning
Está detenido .... You are under arrest.
Está borracho .... You are drunk.

Se prohibe .... It is illegal to ...
Por favor, déjeme ir esta vez .... Please let me go this time.
La mordida, el soborno .... Bribe (not recommended but often practiced).
Enséneme sus papeles .... Let me see your papers.
Seguros .... Insurance
Tuve un accidente .... I had an accident.
Llame una ambulancia .... Call an ambulance.
Llame una grúa .... Call a tow truck.
Se prohibe estacionar .... No parking.
Parquímetro .... Parking meter
Quiero reportar un robo, crimen .... I want to report a robbery, theft.
Quiero ver un abogado, su jefe .... I want to see a lawyer, your boss.
Conozco mis derechos .... I know my rights.

LODGING

Quisiera un cuarto solo .... Single room
Quisiera un cuarto para dos personas .... Double room
Un cuarto al frente .... A front room
Un curato al fondo .... A back room
Camas gemelas .... Twin beds
Camas individuales .... Single beds
¿Hay aire acondicionado? .... Is there air conditioning?
¿Hay agua corriente .... Is there running water?
¿Cuánto cuesta por noche? .... How much per night?
¿Acepta cheques de viajero? .... Do you take traveller's checks?
¿Hay garaje? .... Is there a garage?
¿Hay guarda, vigilante? .... Is there a guard?
Despiérteme a las .... Wake me at
Me quedo _ días .... I'm staying ___ days.
Gerente .... Manager
La carmarera .... Maid
La recepción .... Desk
Piscina, Alberca (Mex.) .... Pool
Agua caliente .... Hot water
Hielo .... Ice
Agua potable .... Drinking water
La cama .... Bed
Tarjeta de Crédito .... Credit card
Dinero en efecto .... Cash
¿Puedo cambiar un cheque de viajero? ... Can I change a travellers check?
¿Cuál es el tipo de cambio? .... What is the rate of exchange?
Me voy, Me marcho .... I'm checking out

La hora de salida .... Check out time
La llave.. Key
Almoada .... Pillow
Toallas .... Towels
Sábanas .... Sheets
Jabón .... Soap
Papel higiénico... Toilet paper
Inodoro .... Toilet
Tender la cama .... Make the bed.
Acensor, Elevador (Mex.) ....Elevator
Escalera .... Stairway
Televisión,tele,televisor .... T.V.

FINDING YOUR WAY

¿Puede indicarme el camino? ....Can you show me the way?
¿Cómo se llega a_____? ....How do you get to_____?
¿Tiene un mapa, plano de____? ....Do you have a map of____?
¿Cuál es la dirección de____? .... What is the address of?
Estoy perdido .... I'm lost
¿A dónde va este camino? .... Where does this road go?
¿Hay_____ por aquí, cerca? .... Is there a _____near by?
¿Es este el camino a_____? .... Is this the road to_____?
¿Voy bien para_____? .... Am I going in the right direction?
¿A qué distancia está_____? .... How far is_____?
¿Está lejos? .... Is it far?
¿Está cerca? .... Is it near?
¿Cuál es el camino más corto? .... What is the shortest way?
¿Cuál es el camino más rápido? .... What is the fastest way?
¿Está en buen estado aquel camino? .... Is that road in good condition?
¿Está pavimentado (or asfaltado) o es de tierra? . Is it paved or is it a dirt road?
¿Hay desviaciones, desvíos? .... Are their detours?
Tramo .... stretch of a road
A la izquierda .... To the left
A la derecha .... To the right
La primera derecha/izquireda .... First right/left
Directo, derecho, recto .... Straight ahead
Más adelante, más allá .... Ahead,beyond
Lo pasó .... You passed it
En el cruce, semáforo .... At the intersection, traffic light

TRAVELING TO MEXICO BY CAR

WHAT YOU NEED BEFORE LEAVING HOME

1. Vehicle registration or Title for your Vehicle. (Bring original and 2 copies).
2. A valid U.S. or Canadian driver's license.
3. Proof of citizenship: Birth Certificate, Voter Registration Card, Passport or Resident Alien Card

WHAT ARE THE PROCEDURES WHEN YOU GET TO THE BORDER

1. Go to the Mexican Customs (Aduana) Vehicle Control Checkpoint
2. Fill out form: TEMPORARY IMPORT PERMIT.
3. Fill out form: VEHICLE RETURN PROMISE AGREEMENT.
4. Fill out form: TOURIST CARD (FMT or FME).
5. Go to Banjérito (Mexican Army Bank) with those three forms.

WHAT OTHER INFORMATION SHOULD YOU KNOW ABOUT DRIVING YOUR CAR TO MEXICO ?

1. You must have these documents with you while driving:
   TEMPORARY IMPORT PERMIT.
   VEHICLE RETURN PROMISE AGREEMENT
   TOURIST CARD (FMT or FME)
   YOUR DRIVER'S LICENSE
   PROOF OF CITIZENSHIP.
   IMPORTANT NOTICE: Do not leave any documents in your unattended vehicle.
2. The temporarily imported vehicle may be driven by another foreigner or Mexican National, as long as the spouse, or any ascendants or decendants of the permit holder is present in the vehicle.
3. Other drivers are allowed only if the permit holder is in the vehicle.

WHAT ARE THE PROCEDURES FOR CROSSING THE BORDER WHEN YOU LEAVE MEXICO ?

1. You must go to any Banjército (Mexican Army Bank) Office.
2. Turn in form: TEMPORARY IMPORT PERMIT and VEHICLE RETURN PROMISE AGREEMENT.
3. Turn in: TOURIST CARD (FTM or FME).
4. Your Vehicle Security Deposit will be returned, or your Bond Agreement, depending which method you used.

IMPORTANT NOTICE

If you are traveling only within the border region (within approximately 15 miles of the border), the Baja California Peninsula, or Sonora Border Region, there is no need to follow any of the procedures contained in this section.

PROCEDURE FOR TEMPORARILY IMPORTING AN AUTOMOBILE INTO MEXICO

In order to bring your car into Mexico, you must complete these forms at the broder:

1. TEMPORARY VEHICLE IMPORT FORM.
2. VEHICLE RETURN PROMISE FORM.
3. TOURIST ENTRY

To complete the above forms, you must bring original and a copy of the following documents with you to the Border:

1. Vehicle Title Registration/License Receipt.
2. Valid Driver's License.
3. Birth Certificate, Passport or Resident Card.

Current Government Regulations require that you post a vehicle bond to insure that your vehicle is returned to your country of origin. There are three (3) options for posting a vehicle bond that must be followed by an American or Canadian citizen or resident who wishes to enter Mexico in a private vehicle.

1. A CREDIT CARD.
2. A VEHICLE VALUE BOND.
       OR
3. A CASH DEPOSIT.

This guide will provide you with all the information you need to bring your vehicle into Mexico. The items in the list above are explained in detail throughout this guide.

CREDIT CARD PROCEDURE

You must have a credit card not issued in Mexico. Only VISA, MasterCard, Diner's Card and American Express cards issued in the name of the person temporarily importing the vehicle will be accepted.

1. IN ORDER TO COMPLETE THESE FORMS YOU MUST HAVE AN ORIGINAL AND A COPY OF THE FOLLOWING DOCUMENTS:

   A. Your Tourist Entry Form (FMT or FME).
   B. The Vehicle Title that shows Legal Ownership of the vehicle and a Registration/License Receipt.

      In the case of a rental vehicle, the rental agreement in the name of the person importing the vehicle.

      In the case of a Company car, furnish a notarized document releasing the vehicle to the interested party and proof of employment.

   C. A valid driver's license not issued in Mexico

   D. A Birth Certificate, Passport or Resident Card.

If you wish to cross the Border in your vehicle, you must have a Temporary Import Application and a Vehicle Return Promise.

These forms are available at the Banco del Ejército offices on the Customs Vehicle Control Checkpoint at the Border or at any Sanborn's or AAA Office in California, Arizona, New Mexico or Texas.

Once you have obtained all these documents and you have completed the Temporary Import Application and the Vehicle Return Promise, you may proceed to the office of the Banco del Ejército. In the event you have not obtained them from the AAA in the U.S.A., go to the Customs Vehicle Control Checkpoint to obtain and complete the Temporary Import Application and the Vehicle Return Promise.

A charge will be made to your International Credit Card for the amount of TWELVE DOLLARS U.S. ($12.00). The voucher can only be filled out and signed in the presence of the Banco del Ejército's personnel at the border crossing and the signature has to be identical to the one on the International Credit Card. No charges will be added to a credit card voucher without first notifying the motorist.

Any additional charges will require documentation on the part of the Mexican Government that the motorist has been officially contacted and given a chance to return their documentation before any charges are levied.

BOND PROCEDURE

Remember, if you already have a copy of the documents mentioned above, but do not have a credit card, or choose not to use one, you may elect to obtain a bond in the name of the Federal Treasury of Mexico. At this time, Mexican bonding companies only operate within the Mexican border, with the exception of Afianzadora Insurgentes, which operate in the U.S. through Sanborn's Insurance of McAllen, Texas. Sanborn's has offices in all of the U.S./Mexican border states.

To obtain a bond, the following is necessary:

1. FURNISH THE BONDING COMPANY WITH THE ORIGINAL AND TWO COPIES OF THE FOLLOWING:

    A. A Resident Card or Passport.
    B. A U.S. Social Security Card.
    C. A valid Driver's License, not issued in Mexico.

    In the event it is a Company vehicle, a Notarized Power of Attorney.

    If the vehicle is not paid in full, you must provide a letter from your financial institution that authorizes you to take the vehicle into Mexico.

2. COST OF THE BOND:

    If the vehicle is a 1988 or older model, the total cost of the bond is One Hundred Twenty-Five U.S. Dollars ($125.00). In the case of all other models, the bond shall cost the equivalent of 1% to 2% of the value of the car plus an issuance fee and taxes. These fees and taxes are not refunded. You are required to pay the deposit in cash (U.S. Dollars) with the Bond Company.

    Be sure to get a receipt for the amount deposited. This amount will be returned to you at any of the Banco del Ejército's offices located in the border crossings, 24 hours a day, in cash U.S. Dollars when you complete your return formalities. **Afianzadora Insurgentes** is the only bonding company that has an arrangement with the Banco del Ejército to return deposits. The other bonding companies return deposits only in their own offices. Please check times and locations for these offices.

Some bonding companies, such as Afianzadora Insurgentes, offer up to 50% discount on the deposit is you present them with an original and 2 copies of your Property Tax Return. However, if you only furnish your Income Tax Return, the discount will be only 30%.

If you own land or real estate in Mexican territory, and you have the proper title with you and furnish the bonding company with a photocopy, the deposit will be One Hundred U.S. Dollars ($100.00).
3. NOTE AND CONTRACTS:

To complete the bond formalities, it is necessary to sign a note and bond application contract.

The bond shall be canceled immediately upon return of the vehicle.

PROCEDURE FOR DEPOSIT AT THE BANCO DEL EJERCITO

If you do not use the credit card procedure, and do not obtain a bond from a Mexican bonding company, you may make a deposit at the Banco del Ejército offices at the border in an amount equal to 100% of the vehicle's value. These transactions cost TWELVE DOLLARS U.S. ($12.00) and have basically the same document requirements as other procedures.

Your deposit will be returned to you in full only upon completing the return formalities at the same office at which the deposit was made. Deposits are returned only between 8:30 a.m. and 3:00 p.m., Monday through Friday.

Vehicle deposit amounts have been approved by the Mexican Treasury as published in the Official Gazette. Deposit amounts vary according to the vehicle type and model.

BOND AND DEPOSIT SCHEDULE

BONDS

VEHICLE TYPE	1	2	3	4
1992-1994	$10,000	$7,500	$6,000	$20,000

1989-1991	7,000	4,000	3,000	12,000
1986-1988	3,000	1,500	1,000	5,000
1980-1985	1,500	1,000	750	3,000
Prior to 1980	500	500	500	1,000

Example of Vehicle Types
1. Luxury Cars such as Grand Marquis, New Yorker, Cadillac, Van, Minivan (any make)
2. Pickups
3. Compact and medium-size cars such as Nissan, VW, Honda, Mitsubishi, Ford, Chevrolet
4. European and sportscars such as Mercedes Benz, BMW, Alfa Romeo, Jaguar, Porsche, Corvette, Trans Am

DEPOSITS

DEPOSIT CHART FOR BOND PROCEDURES

Type	1994-1992 Deposit Amount	1991-1989 Deposit Amount	1988-1986 Deposit Amount	1985-1981 Deposit Amount	1980-x Deposit Amount
Luxury Van Minivan	$10,000-5,000	$7,000-3,500	$3,000-1,500	$1,500-750	$500-250
European Japanese Sportscar	20,000-10,000	12,000-6,000	5,000-2,500	3,000-1,500	1,000-500
Compact Midsize	6,000-3,000	3,000-1,500	1,000-500	750-375	500-250
Pickups	7,500-3,750	4,500-2,000	1,500-750	1,000-500	500-250

All Amounts in U.S. Dollars

HOURS OF OPERATION
BANJERCIO (BANCO DEL EJERCITO)

CALIFORNIA BORDER CITIES	HOURS
Mexicali	Daily 24HRS
Tecate	Daily 8 AM - 4 PM
Tijuana	Mon.-Fri. 8 AM - 9 PM

Saturday, 8 AM - 5 PM

ARIZONA BORDER CITIES	HOURS
Agua Prieta	Daily 24 HRS
Naco	Daily 8 AM - 12 Midnight
Nogales	Daily 24 HRS
San Luis Rio Colorado	Daily 24 HRS
Sonoyta	Daily 24 HRS

TEXAS BORDER CITIES	HOURS
Ciudad Acuña	Daily 24 HRS
Ciudad Juarez	Daily 24 HRS
Ciudad Miguel Alemán	Daily 24 HRS
Columbia	Mon.-Fri. 10 AM - 6 PM
General Rodrigo M. Quevedo	Daily 24 HRS
Matamoros	Daily 24 HRS
Nuevo Laredo	Daily 24 HRS
Ojinaga	Mon.-Fri. 7:30 AM - 4 PM
	Saturday, 7:30 AM - 4 PM
	Sunday, 8 AM - 4 PM
Piedras Negras	Mon.-Fri. 8 AM - 8 PM
	Saturday, 10 AM - 2 PM
Puerto Palomas	Daily 24 HRS
Reynosa	Daily 24 HRS

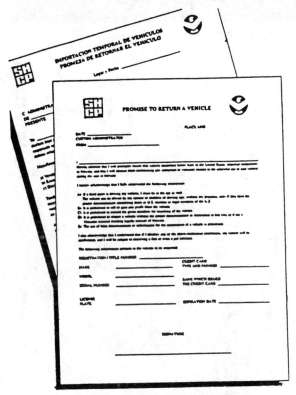

IMPORTANT

It is very important to remember the following:

1. The Vehicle Import Permit is valid for up to six (6) months.

2. The temporarily imported vehicle may be driven multiple times across the border during the authorized period.

3. While driving in Mexico, always carry the Vehicle Import Permit with you.

4. If you ar leaving Mexico and do not plan to return during the 6 month authorized period, you must cancel the Vehicle Import Permit at the Banco del Ejército. Otherwise, you may encounter problems when you try to re-enter Mexico at a future time.

MEXICO ROUTE MAP

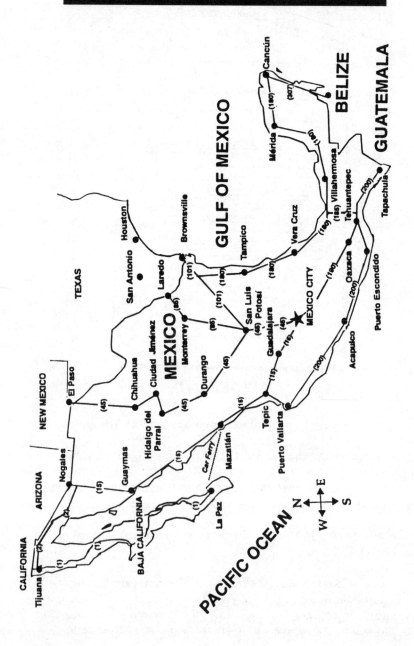

MEXICO

When you head south into Mexico, if you plan to continue on into Central America, you will have several choices of routes to take. The maps on pages 20 and 21, and the map of Mexico on page 46 will give you a breakdown of the most prominent cities along each route.

Mexico is a part of North America, and stretches from the U. S. border on the north, the Pacific Ocean on the west, the Gulf of Mexico to the east, and Belize and Guatemala on the south. On the routes along each coast, which are at or near sea level, you can expect to find temperatures in the 90 to 100 degree range during the days, with humidity quite high. The routes in the center of the country start at near 3,500 to 3,700 feet of elevation, climbing to over 7,000 feet in Mexico City. At those elevations, you can expect to find more moderate temperatures in the 60 to 80 degree range. Because of hot summer temperatures and many desolate stretches of highway, we don't recommend you travel by Mexico's Highway (1) down the Baja Peninsula to La Paz and then take the ferry to Mazatlán.

If your itinerary allows you the luxury of sightseeing, some of the most prominent places of interest, from north to south, are:

(1) WEST COAST ROUTE - FROM NOGALES, AZ
HERMOSILLO is the Capital of the northern state of Sonora. The city has a beautiful twin-towered Cathedral built in 1821, plus an array of interesting buildings including museums and the University of Sonora. This city is popular with travellers along Mexico's West Coast because it has all the conveniences of a modern city.
GUAYMAS located on the Gulf of California, is one of Mexico's finest sea ports, with good fishing and excellent beaches.
MAZATLAN about 500 miles to the south is opposite the tip of Baja California and has auto ferry service to and from La Paz. This port offers numerous hotels, motels and trailer parks of all price ranges, sightseeing, fishing and beach activities. Travellers will notice that the vegetation starts to becomes more tropical just north of Mazatlán. This is because this port lies just below the Tropic of Cancer.
PUERTO VALLARTA is a once-sleepy seaport which became a tourist resort after the publicity given to it by the "Liz" Taylor/Richard Burton filming of *The Night of the Iguana*. It is one of the West Coast's favorite resorts, with deep-sea fishing, water sports and sightseeing cruises. An excursion to the nearby fishing village of Yelapa is worth your while.

ACAPULCO, is one of the most popular and beautiful beach resorts in North America. It has hotels of every price range, restaurants and RV facilities. It offers big game fishing, water sports, bullfights, discoteques, great nightlife, plenty of picturesque scenry, tennis, golf, spectacular cliff divers, horseback riding and has long been a favorite with the "Jet Set". Check out the sunsets at Pie de La Cuesta northwest of the city.

PUERTO ESCONDIDO or small port in Spanish, is a good spot to layover between Acapulco and the Mexico/Guatemala border. This beach town remains charmingly quaint despite recent development in the area. Puerto Angel, several hours to the south, is another nice fishing village.

TAPACHULA near the Mexico/Guatemala border, has good hotels and motels and a convenient stopover prior to entering Central America.

(2) BORDER CROSSING AT NOGALES, AZ

Follow Route #1 past Mazatlán to Tepic, then to Guadalajara.

GUADALAJARA is Mexico's second largest city, and favorite retirement haven for *"gringos"*. Its 5,000 foot elevation affords a temperate climate for comfortable living. The city offers many beautiful buildings, sightseeing tours, museums, shopping, bullfights, and a full range of sports. One could spend a week here and not cover everything there is to see or do. Nearby Lake Chapala is a popular area with retirees. (For those continuing to Southern Mexico and/or Central America, continue to Mexico City and join route #4 from Laredo to Central America).

(3) BORDER CROSSING FROM EL PASO, TX

CHIHUAHUA is noted as the home of the Mexican Chihuahua dogs, as well as its silver mines and lumber mills. Its greatest attraction is the train trip to the famed **"Copper Canyon"**, which is said to be more spectacular than the Grand Canyon. The trip to Los Mochis on the Gulf of California takes some 14 hours. Also, about 19 miles from the city, one can explore spectacular **Cumbres de Majalaca National Park** with its spectacular geological formations. It offers lodging, camping and food. This area is very hot in the summer and can drop to freezing temperatures on winter nights.

DURANGO is a good overnight stop. There is a lot of sightseeing available, including movie sets that are used for filming Westerns. This is where John Wayne had his movie-set ranch. From Durango, your route can take you to Mazatlán to join the Pacific Coast route, or to San Luis Potosí to join the Laredo to Mexico City route.

(4) CROSSING THE BORDER AT LAREDO, TX

MONTERREY, NUEVO LEON is Mexico's third largest city, and is an easy drive from San Antonio, Texas. A city of both light and heavy industry, it has abundant hotels, motels and RV parks. It offers much to see in the way of palaces, museums and parks, as well as golf, bullfights and other sports.

SAN LUIS POTOSI was originally established as a mining town. It is has numerous hotels, motels and RV accommodations. Like most large cities in Mexico, it has museums, cathedrals, and other sightseeing.

QUERETARO is a city noted for its historical role in the development of Mexico from the 1500s into the 20th century. Of interest is its six-mile-long aqueduct that is still in use 200 years after it was built.

MEXICO CITY, D.F. is the largest city in Mexico and its capital. It is worthy of a long visit to absorb all of its archaeological sights, museums and palaces. The city's elevation ranges from 7,200 to 8,000 feet, covering some 1800 square miles. A large part of the valley was originally a large lake bed, giving the city a very unstable foundation and making it subject to disastrous damage during its frequent earthquakes. Mexico City was the adopted home of the Aztec Indians who settled in Chapultepec in the 13th century. The original natives of the area, who lived in "city/states" that were each ruled by a king, did not like these invaders because of their religion of eating human hearts during their religious ceremonies. They drove the Aztecs out to one of the areas where the University of Mexico now stands. From their base on an island of Lake Texcoco, the Aztecs launched attacks on the other cities of the area, until by 1428 they controlled the entire area. By the 16th century, their conquests had expanded to include all of Mexico. When Hernan Cortés landed in Mexico in 1519 looking for gold and silver, he began to conquer the Aztecs. By 1521, he had captured all of the Aztec holdings. Today you can still see some of vestiges of the different pre-Colombian peoples who lived in the area of Mexico City:

Teotihuacán was the center of power in the area from 100 A.D. until destroyed in 750 A.D. The huge pyramids and plazas are still there.

Texcoco was prominent in pre-Columbian times. The remains of hilltop gardens and aqueduct system are still visible.

Xochimilco Gardens date from the time of the Aztecs and is made up of clumps of floating surface vegetation held in place by being anchored to trees, with colorful floating gardens of flowers. You can view all of this if you take a gondola ride.

The **Popocapetetl** (Smoking Mountain) and **Ixataccihualtl** (Sleeping Woman) volcanoes, are highly visible towering over the Mexico City area. Other interesting sights include **The Alameda** and **Chapultepec** parks. While at the latter park be sure to visit the Castle of Cahpultepec, which was once the seat of the Aztec rulers, and is now a museum that contains relics of the Emperor Maximillian and his wife Carlotta. Another "must' is the **Museo Nacional de Antropología**. It is filled with pre-Columbian artefacts and is considered one of the best museums in the world. You will need a couple of days to see everything.

PUEBLA located just two hours from Mexico City, it is a city that should interest visitors. One place that draws many tourists is the Talavera Tile Works, where colorful tile and ceramics are molded and painted by hand, then fired and cooled as you watch. The streets are crowded and narrow, so it may be advisable to leave your car at your hotel and take a bus. Other items of interest are pottery, carved onyx ornaments, furniture, candy shops and delicious cuisine. **CUERNAVACA** is one of the most beautiful cities in Mexico, and just a short drive from Mexico City. A drive through the colorful residential neighborhood is well worth your while. If you are fortunate to be there on a Thursday of one of the first three months of the year, many of the homes are open to the public. This has been a favorite summer retreat for the rulers and the wealthy from the time of Cortés. There are many museums including the former home of Cortés, and several Aztec pyramids in the area.

OAXACA is a colorful city was founded by Cortés in 1529 and has maintained its original Indian influence over the years. Shoppers will delight in the local-made leather goods, jewelry, hand carved handles of the Oaxacan knives with etched blades. If you are there on a Saturday, don't miss the "Mercado de Abastos", a 10 square block area where Indians from the surrounding villages come to sell their wares. In the evenings, plan to have your dinner at the Zócalo (Central Plaza) where many sidewalk restaurants serve fine cuisine to the accompaniment of Mariachi bands.

TAPACHULA is the last Mexican city you will have to pass through if you are planning to drive to Guatemala and into Central America. See page 52 for travelling through Guatemala.

(5)BORDER CROSSING AT BROWNSVILLE, TX

You have two choices here: If you want to take the shortest and fastest route to Guatemala and limit your driving time in Mexico, take gulf route (6) from Brownsville. But if you are planning to drive at a higher elevation along the central route, you will head inland from Bownsville towards San Luis Potosí. So, please refer to route #4 on page 49 and pick up this route at San Luis Potosí.

(6) BORDER CROSSING AT BROWNSVILLE, TX

TAMPICO is a seaport town with oil refineries on the Gulf Coast. Fishing is its greatest tourist attraction.

VERACRUZ is Mexico's principal port of entry on the Gulf of Mexico. It is noted for its cigars, coffee and seafood. Veracruz has been the invasion route into Mexico since the time of Cortés in 1519. Pirates, slave traders, the French troops in 1860, the U.S. forces in the Mexican-American War of 1846-1848 and again in 1914, all used this route to enter Mexico. Sidewalk cafes in the heart of the city, around the Plaza de Armas, are active in the evening for dinner and listening to the famous *Jarocho* harp music of this area.

ACAYUCAN is the best place to cross over the Isthmus of Tehuantepec westward from the east coast to the Pan-American Highway (200) and on into Central America. If you are going to the Yucatan Peninsula, continue to:

VILLAHERMOSA, founded by Cortés in 1519, was a seaport for exporting rubber, cocoa and coffee. Lately it has become a center for exporting oil from its rich oil fields. Mayan ruins abound in the surrounding area and are within driving distance of the city. **Comalcalco**, consists of the ruins of several temples and tombs. **Palenque**, located nearby, has some of the best preserved ruins in Mexico. There are also several museums in the area filled with artifacts from the Mayan era.

MERIDA is the site of an ancient Mayan city. It is the capital of the state of Yucatan and has been given the name "The Paris of the Western World", with many European-type homes, some made of Carrara marble. Horsedrawn carriages take you sightseeing in the downtown area, where there are many fine restaurants, museums and art galleries.

CHICHEN ITZA is considered an archaeological wonder which has been partially restored. It was believed to have been built between 350 and 450 A.D. and has a nine level pyramid, the Court of the Thousand Columns, and many temples. If interested in exploring this area, you should hire a guide and allow at least two or three days.

CANCUN is located on white coral sand beaches with a row of hotels at the water's edge. It has become the main tourist attraction on the Yucatán Peninsula. The **Cobá** area , south of Cancún, is a classical Maya city aand ceremonial center and has more than 6500 buildings dating from 600 to 900 A.D. It also has a 138 foot high pyramid.

CHETUMAL, is located near the border of Belize, and on the only overland route to Belize from Mexico. Near this city are more Mayan ruins for you to explore.

(7) FROM TAPACHULA, MEXICO TO PANAMA CITY, PANAMA
On the following pages will be outlines of the countries of Central America. You may follow the order as listed on page 23.

GUATEMALA ROUTE MAP

PACIFIC OCEAN

GUATEMALA

As you drive south from Mexico, the first country in Central America you encounter will be Guatemala. It is the northernmost country of Central America, and is bordered by Mexico to the north, Belize and the Caribbean to the east, Honduras and El Salvador to the south and the Pacific Ocean to the west.

Guatemala is divided by the Sierra Madre mountains along the Pacific, and the Cuchumatanes Mountains which run across the country to the Caribbean. Other mountain ranges are the Sierra de Chama, the Sierra de Chuacus and the Merendon Range. Within these mountains are more than 30 volcanoes, which rise above the surrounding terrain. Many are active and send up high plumes of smoke. Those of you who love to hike, can climb their lofty slopes. The views of the countryside are exhilarating. If you do decide to climb one of the country's volcanoes, it is recommended you go with a group of people, make sure you know the safest trails, and have warm clothing and waterproof gear in the rainy season. You should also hire an experienced guide. Many of the more popular ones are:

The **Pacay Volcano** (8370 ft. above sea level), located south of spectacularly beautiful Lake Amatitlán. From San Francisco de Sales, it takes about 4 hours to reach the summit lakes and the active Mackenny crater where you can photograph its boiling lava.

The **Agua Volcano** (12,349 ft.). From the town of Santa María de Jesús, which is about 11 miles from the colorful and interesting city of Antigua, one can climb this awesome volcano. The view from its crater is spectacular, and includes the western mountain ranges as well as all of Southern Guatemala.

The **Acatengo Volcano** (13,349 ft.) and the **Fuego Volcano** (12,342 ft.) are located west of La Antigua. The cone of Fuego was destroyed during an eruption in 1962, and still smokes and spews ashes and sand. Starting from the town of Acatenango, one is able to climb both volcanoes on one hike.

The **Atitlán Volcano** (11,598 ft.), the **Tolimán Volcano** (10,280 ft.) and the **San Pedro Volcano** (9,905 ft.) encircle Lake Atitlán. It takes about 8 hrs. to climb Atitlán, 6 hrs. to climb Tolimán and 5 hrs. for San Pedro. All of these volcanoes afford a panoramic view of Lake Atitlán— one of the world's most beautiful lakes.

Numerous rivers flow from the two main mountain ranges of Guatemala. Those on the Pacific watershed have many rapids and spectacular waterfalls. These rivers include the **Suchiate, Naranjo, Samala, Michatoya, Paz** and **Los Esclavos**. On the Caribbean watershed, the main rivers are **Usumacinta, La Pasión, Salinas** and the **Río Azul** (or **Río Hondo**). These rivers offer white water rafting and fishing, as well as an abundance of tropical birds and animals.

Guatemala's numerous lakes, many of which are of volcanic origin, make for great fishing and water sports. The major ones include **Atitlán, Amatitlán, Izabel, Petén, Itza, Guija** and **Ayarza**.

The climate of Guatemala averages about 75 degrees (F.). Temperatures hover at around 100 degrees in the coastal and low-lying areas to near freezing in the highlands. As in most of Central America, the rainy season lasts from May through October. During this period you will find sunny mornings with clear blue skies. The clouds start forming near mid-day, and the rains last, usually, a couple of hours in late afternoon or evening. As the sun sets, the skies usually clear, revealing a brilliant display of sparkling stars and fireflies. The whole countryside turns a dark shade of green during the wet season.

One of the main reasons to visit Guatemala is to see the numerous vestiges of the ancient Mayan civilization which flourished in this area long before Columbus discovered the new world. The Mayans were a very intelligent race, excelling in astronomy, medicine, mathematics, agriculture, politics and religion.

The population of Guatemala, in most cases, is a mixture of the native Indians and Spaniards, plus many ethnic groups who are descendants of the original Mayans. The conquest of the country by the Spaniards began in the early 16th century and lasted until the end of the 17th century. Spain granted Guatemala, as well as the other Central American countries, its independence on September 15, 1821. From 1821 until July 1, 1847, it was annexed to Mexico. After 1847 it was established as a republic, and remains so today. It now has a popularly elected president, a congress and a judicial branch. It consists of 22 departments, equivalent to states in the United States. Recently Guatemalans had reason to celebrate. A peace accord was signed by representatives of the government and the leaders of the guerilla insurgency after nearly thiry years of civil war and a loss of around 150,000 lives. This sad chapter in Guatemalan history is now closed and the country looks forward to growth as the new century approaches.

The major source of the country's income is coffee, followed by cotton, cocoa, corn, beans, bananas, sugar cane, vegetables, flowers and fruit. Recently, cattle, tourism, manufacturing, industry and foreign trade have increased and now also play a major role in the economy. Guatemala is also noted for brilliantly colored woven textiles. Indian women produce beautifully embroidered blouses, skirts and other articles. They may be purchased at most marketplaces like Chichicastenango. Some Indian women spend months working on a particular design.

Recently, there has been an increase in the number of foreigners living in Guatemala. They are taking advantage of the low cost of living and good weather. Guatemala has copied Costa Rica's former *Pensionado* status to attract potential retirees. The cost of living is so low, a single person can live or retire in Gualtemala for well under $1,000 per month.

Like Costa Rica, the Guatemalan people are very loving and friendly. This another reason to consider living in Guatemala. If you interested in living ors retiring in Guatemala , contact:

GUATEMALA TOURIST COMMISSION,
7a Avenida 1-17, Zone 4, Centro Cívico
Guatemala City, Guatemala, C.A.
Tel: (502) 231 1333
FAX: (502) 231 8893 or (502) 231 4416

GUATEMALA - TOURIST ATTRACTIONS

GUATEMALA CITY is the capital of the country. It is the largest city in Central America and has over 2,000,000 people. The city offers a variety of accomodations, restaurants, old churches, English book-stores, historic buildings, many museums and a whole lot more. The **Mercado Central** is a good place to purchase tourist-oriented items such as handicrafts and hand woven textiles. The **Mapa En Relieve** (a giant relief map) and Minerva Park are two places tourists visit. Gualtemala City is a good layover spot on the Pan-American Highway (CA-1). You can take a few extra days to explore nearby areas, lakes and even make an excursion to the Mayan sites. In general, Guatemala is an excellent country for sightseeing.

ANTIGUA, is a city of 30,000 and is 45 minutes from Guatemala City. It was the former capital until it was heavily damaged by earthquakes. Here you can watch the Indian women weave the uniquely colorful and beautiful fabrics native to Guatemala. Many Spanish-built structures, such as the Palace of the Captains General, La Concepción and Capuchinas Convents and the Popence House have been restored to their original splendor after damage by earthquakes. Because of the dozens of Spanish language schools in this city, there is always a large number of foreigners. Antigua's is one of "the" places to go outside of the U.S. to study Spanish. You can study as many hours a day as you wish. There are all types of programs to suite everyone's needs. You can even live with a local family to really immerse yourself in the culture.

CHICHICASTENAGO, a most colorful town located very high in the mountains about 87 miles from Guatemala City, is a highly recommended side trip. Every Thursday and Sunday the Indians bring their wares to the central market square. They are all dressed in the colorful woven costumes of their home village, each with the distinctive patterns of that village. Their wares include weavings, wood carvings, ceramics and local fruits and produce. All of this is held in the square with the backdrop of Santo Tomás church. If you want to stay by Lake Atitlán there is a bus from nearby Panajachel to Chichicastenango. The highway passes through some lovely landscape.

LAKE ATITLAN, Sololá. This lake, some 90 miles from Guatemala City is renowned for its natural beauty. There are three volcanoes surrounding the lake: Volcán Tolimán, Volcán Atitlán and Volcán San Pedro. Tourists are attracted to the colorful Indian settlements along the lake shore, fishing and swimming in the lake's peaceful waters, and to climb the surrounding volcanoes. The most polular town on the lake is Panajachel nicknamed "Gringolandia" because of the many foreigners who visit or live in the area. There are some watersports available there.

The view of the lake with the volcanoes in the background make this place really magical. The temperature is about 70 degress all year long making it an ideal place to live. You can take a small launch from the lake front and visit several other towns located around the lake. The Indian village of Santiago de Atitlán on the opposite of the lake is the most frequently visited village after Panajachel. There is a national park in this area and you can even go on an excursion to one of the volcanoes. If you are in good shape you can climb one of these volcanoes. The view from the top of Lake Atilán is almost worth the effort. This area is perhaps the most beautiful spot in Central America let alone the rest of the world.

RIO DULCE, Izabel, some 170 miles from Guatemala City is the place for the adventurous and nature lovers. Of particular interest are Lake Izabel, the town of Livingston, the Fort of San Felipe built in Colonial times and the Caribbean beaches of **Cocoli** and **Costa de Palma**.

GUATEMALA - ARCHEOLOGICAL SITES

Tikal, El Petén National Park. This is the home of the Mayan civilization, which was the greatest civilization in the Western Hemisphere starting in a period some 2500 years ago. Found here are important temples, carvings, dwellings and examples of Mayan mathematical and astronomical knowledge. The city was mysteriously abandoned around the year 900 A.D., and the wild animals, birds and jungles reclaimed it for many years. From Guatemala City, you take a 30 minute flight or 24 hour drive over bad roads to Flores, which is close to Tikal. Lodging and guides are available there.

Ceibal, El Petén, first settled around 800 B.C. is often called the "Mayan Art Gallery" because of its well preserved sculptures and pottery.

Yaxha, El Petén, is a city that was laid out in a street network similar to today's city blocks.

Uaxatun, El Petén, existed longer than any other Mayan city. Its writing system and calendar originated here.

El Mirador, El Petén, which is located just four miles from the Mexican border is under excavation, so special permits may be needed to explore this site.

El Naranjo, El Petén, contains many impressive structures such as the hieroglyphic stairway and ball court.

Quirigua, Izabel, contains the largest block of stone ever quarried by the Mayas. It is made of sandstone and measures 35 feet long by 5 feet wide and weighs some 65 tons.

BELIZE ROUTE MAP

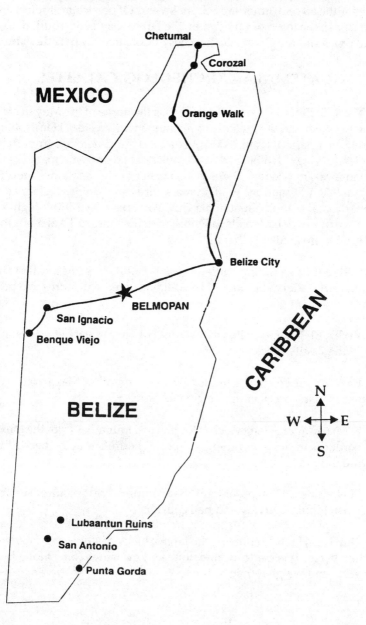

BELIZE

Belize, formerly known as British Honduras, borders on Mexico and Guatemala, and comprises a area of about 9,000 square miles. Its greatest length is about 175 miles north to south. Its widest point is about 70 miles.

It is the only country where English is the official primary language. The largest ethnic group in the country are the Black Creoles who speak Creole English or their own dialect. Spanish is the popular second language. During the 1700s, Britain settled into the country, and in 1862, declared it a colony of Great Britain. Due to economic and political pressures, on September 21, 1981 Britain loosened its hold, and Belize was declared an independent nation. Guatemala had always considered Belize as one of its "departments" (states), but in 1991, Belize was formally recognized as an independent nation.

The Northern coastal plain of Belize is swampy, flat and hot. Along the Western edge of the country are the Maya mountains with lush growth up to its 3,000 foot elevation. The Southern section is low, hot and humid with an abundance of rainfall like most other costal areas. Along the off-shore coast are many islands called **"Cayes"** (pronounced keys), and the longest barrier reef in the Western hemisphere (the fifth longest coral barrier reef after Australia's Great Barrier Reef). It has become a popular place for scuba divers, as miles of the reef are only about 15 feet deep out to the cayes. This area is rapidly becoming a tourist mecca, which is a valuable asset for the economy of the country.

The country's good weather, lovely beaches, sparkling clear 85 degree water, easy immigration laws and residency requirements and low cost of living have made the country a mecca for foreigners. Like Guatemala and Costa Rica, Belize has an expatriate community. If you are interested we suggest you read "The Belize Retirement Guide" we list in the back of this book.

Presently, forestry is the major source of income, although sugar growing and processing is a very important source that contributes to the economy of Belize.

Belize City is the Country's largest city and has a population of around 70,000. It was the capital until 1961 when a major hurricane destroyed a large part of the city. It was then decided to move the capital to another location that was not so much at the mercy of hurricanes. A new capitol was built in Belmopan, which is located almost in the center of the country. However, Belize City is still considered the country's main city. The city itself is not very attractive and with its wooden houses and is really nothing more than an overgrown shanty town. It has its share of hotels, restaurants, bars and night spots. There is a lot of theft, so watch your belongings.

Belize City still has some consulates, although there is a move for them to relocate in the new capital of the country. If you plan to drive from Belize to Guatemala, be sure to obtain your visa for Guatemala before arriving in Belize. You still have time to get it before you leave Mexico, as there is a Guatemalan Embassy in Chetumal, Mexico, right on the Mexican-Belize border.

The Cayes (pronounced "keys") are the many islands that are off-shore along the coast of Belize. There are over 212 square miles of cayes. The two most popular ones are **Caye Cauker** and **Ambergris Caye**. Caye Cauker, is the less expensive of the two. This tiny island lies only 21 miles from Belize City. It is your basic affordable tropical island paradise with a permanent population of under 1000 people. Fishing, specifically loberstering, is the main industry of this small island but tourism is on the rise. There is great scuba diving, with underwater visibility some 50 to 75 yards. There are underwater caves that are very interesting as well as challenging, but you should have an experienced guide with you. Check with the dive shops for both the necessary equipment and guides. Because the water on the west side of the cayes is so shallow—averaging about 15 feet— it is quite warm. Beaches are practically non-existent, so sun bathing is best on the docks or in the deck chairs of your hotel. This small island boasts a large number of small cafes and restaurants.

Ambergris Caye is the largest of the cayes. and the most popluated and developed. Its principal town is San Pedro which has a populaion of 2,000. For years this town has been the main tourist attraction of Belize. It has become the hideaway for the Europen "Jet-Set" and was even featured on the program "Lifestyles of the Rich and Famous." Prices are slightly higher than at Caye Caulker, but are still a good vacation bargain.

The diving here is first-rate with some of the most beautiful underwater scenery in the world. Sponges and coral abound and the visibility is extraordinary most of the year. The nearby Belize reef is littered with shipwrecks and a great place to explore. You can even take diving lessons at one of the many dive shops in the area. If you want to stay on land there are areas where you can beachcomb for shells. There are over 50 hotels, discos and bars with good nightlife. Information on hotels, restaurants and equipment rental may be found in the guidebooks: *Central America on a Shoestring, The Belize Retirement Guide* and *The New Key to Belize*. See the ad at the end of this book for more details about these guidebooks.

Belmopan is a new city that was built to become the capital after Hurricane Hattie in 1961. It is located in the geographical center of the country and 50 miles from Belize City. The population is only 4000 and there isn't a whole lot to do at night. It is a complietely planned city with no wooden structures permitted. Nearby Guanacaste Park nature preserve is a nice excursion. The Department of Archaeology is a building where tourists can view Mayan artefacts.

Many Mayan artefacts have been found in Belize's Mayan Ruins. Major Mayan sites include **Xuantunich** ('Maiden of the Rock'), the most important site located located in southern Belize on the Mayan route to the Caribbean from Tikal, Guatemala. There are classical Mayan ruins found there with beautiful surroundings. In southern Belize are the ruins of **Lubanntun**.('Fallen Stones') This site dates from about 900A.D. and was the major cermonial site in southern Belize. It is from the late Mayan period and therefore considered unique. Eleven main structures are grouped around five main plazas. There are also three ball courts. The tallest structure rises 50 feet above the plaza, from which you can see the Caribbean Sea. More Mayan sites ahve recently been discovered, like Uxbenka found in 1984. There are other new sites being unearthered which should be of interested to travellers interested in the Mayan Civilization. Archaeologists say that Belize's forests still contain hundreds of unexcavated Mayan sites.

When crossing the border to Guatemala, the town nearest the border on the Belize side is **Benque Viejo del Carmen**. The borders are usually open from 8 a.m. to noon and 2 to 6p.m. You can get through during the off hours but will be charged an extra fee. Money may also be exchanged before crossing into Guatemala or on the other side of the border. On the Guatemalan side is the city of **Melchor de Mencos**, where you will clear customs into the country of Guatemala. Like other border crossings be sure all of your papers are in order to avoid delays. Don't forget to read our section on border crossings Apply the same general rules and common sense when entering Belize from Mexico via Chetumal and exiting the country.

EL SALVADOR ROUTE MAP

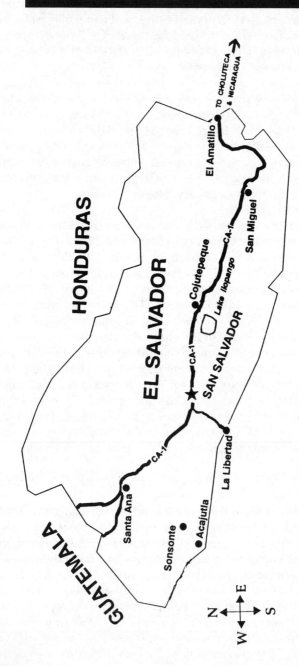

EL SALVADOR

Located with Guatemala to the west, Honduras to the north and east, and the Pacific Ocean to the south, is El Salvador. El Salvador is smallest and most densly populated of the Central American countries. There are around a five million warm and friendly people who live in its 8,203 square miles of scenic country. Like other countries in Central America, it has warm temperatures along its coastline and cooler temperatures in the higher mountain regions. From about May through October is the rainy season here, with the dry season extending from November through April. The country's land is very fertile and ripe for all types of agriculture and like most of the other central American countries has its share of volcanoes.

The warm tropical climate, fertile volcanic soil and lush vegetation make the country a veritable paradise. Besides rich farmlands, you will see a myriad of brilliantly colored flowers and trees full of blossoms which are a sight to behold.

El Salvador's earliest civilization can be traced back 3,500 years to 1,500 B.C. as many pre-Columbian artifacts attest to. Long before the Spanish conquerors came in 1524, this country had developed its many customs, dances and ceremonies, as well as the highly evolved cermonial centers which have been unearthed. Some of the most prominent archaeological sites are **Tazumal** and **San Andrés**. The step pryamid ruins at these sites testify to the Mayan presence in western El Salvador that lasted over 1000 years. Evidence of both the decendents of the Toltec and Aztec tribes of Mexico is also present. **Joya de Ceren** which was discovered in 1976 is another interesting Mayan site.

Each city, village and hamlet celebrates the protection of its Patron Saint with colorful festivities every year. Some of the famous festivities occur in Santa Ana in July, Santa Cruz de Roma in September, San Miguel with its famous colorful carnival on November 24th, Sonsonate in February and Panchimalco in May, just to name a few. During these and on other celebrations, you will see the traditional folklorical dances that originated in the pre-Columbian era and are mixed with Spanish influence. Dancers dressed up with masks and very colorful clothes, coins, feathers and other decorative ornaments.

Salvadorians are very creative as witnessed by their typical art and crafts made of every imaginable material, including twigs, clay, fabrics, wood, bamboo and palm tree branches. Some of the places noted for their crafts are: Nahuizalco for its twigged furniture; Ilobasco for its ceramics; San Sebastian for its *"colchas"* and hammocks; Tenancingo for its *"sombreros"* (hats) and La Palma and Chalatenango for their assortment of treasures which are known worldwide for their beauty and originality.

El Salvador's official currency is the *colón* which has a floating value against the dollar. The rate is published daily in the newspapers. There are numerous banks where you can exchange your dollars and travellers checks, as well as in hotels and other places of business.

SAN SALVADOR is the capital of El Salvador, largest and most important city in the country, and is one of the most modern cities in Central America. Located at an elevation of 2,300 feet, it boasts a wonderful year-round climate. The city sits in a valley at the foot of the large San Salvador volcano and has around 500,000 inhabitants. Since its "Civil War", it has flowered into an ideal city of contrasting beauty, sprinkled with the old buildings and modern skyscrapers of the 21st Century. There are many modern hotels and exquisite restaurants to pamper your stay in this city of hospitality. There are a number of good bars, cafés and plenty of nightlife to keep you busy. While in El Salvador you should try *pupasas*, the most popular dish of the country. They are two corn tortillas stuck together with cheese or meat in the center. Typical handicrafts can be purchased at one of the cites two main markets. There is a zoo, musuems and colonial buildings you can visit when sightseeing. Your cultural side will enjoy the theater, art shows and modern dancing co-mingled with expressions of folkloric dances.

The county has a couple of nice fresh water lakes where you may take part in watersports or just relax. About 10 miles east of San Salvador is the **Lago de Ilopango**. It is the largest lake in the country and about 10 miles long and 3 miles wide. You may takes boat rides, sun youself, swim in the lake or enjoy the local lake fish at one of the restaurants in around the lake. There are also a few hotels if you wish to spend the night near the lake. Located just off Central American Highway (1) is **Lake Coatepeque**. It is another favorite weekend resort with good sailing and fishing near the foot of Santa Ana volcano.

Just a half-hour's drive from San Salvador are the warm, sparkling waters of the Pacific and many fine beaches that make up the 188 mile coastline of El Salvador. From **Garitis Palmera** beach near the Guatemalan border, to **La Barra de Santiago** beach, **Las Cobanos, El Majahual, Conchalito, La Zunganera, Costa del Sol, La Herradura, Estero de Jaltepeque, Jiquilisco, El Espino** and **El Cuco** to **El Tamarindo** beach on the Gulf of Fonesca, you will find a myraid of sun-drenched pristine beaches for your tanning and swimming pleasure. Surfers will enjoy the huge waves all along the coastline.

The seaside fishing town of **La Libertad** is the closest beach to the capital. Because it is only 22 miles from the San Salvador it is very popular with the locals on weekends and holidays. There is a black sand beach and the surf can be very strong. Accomodations are plentiful. There are also open-air restaurants along the beach where you can savor all types of delicious seafood.

La Libertad is conveniently located along Central America Highway-2 or CA-2 on most maps which runs along the coast. So, if you choose to take the costal route, you can stop and have lunch here or even spend the night. **Zunzal** to the west has some of the best surfing beaches in Central America.

El Salvador's volcanoes contribute to the rugged landscape of the country. One of the most visible is the **Izcalco Volcano**, a perfect cone of black lava some 6,183 feet high, which can be viewed from **Cerro Verde** (Green Hill) where you may enjoy the hospitality of the Hotel de La Montaña (Hotel of the Mountain).

The country has a couple of nice national parks. The **Montecristo** cloud forest is an international nature reserve. However, you can visit it only during certain times of the year since it is protected.

La Carretera Panorámica (Panoramic Highway)is a scenic road between the Pan-American Highway CA-1 and Highway CA-8, is famous for its fantastic views and scenery. It passes by one side of Coatepeque Lake.

Because this counry is so small, you can conceivably enjoy the city of San Salvador, have lunch at the seashore and spend the night at a fascinating lakeview hotel high on the slopes of a volcano—all in one day.

HONDURAS ROUTE MAP

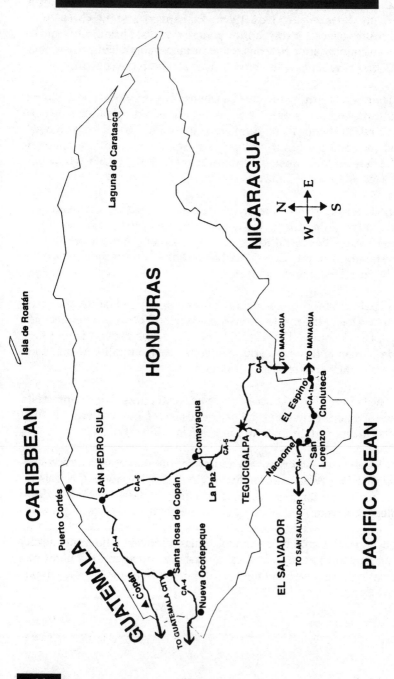

HONDURAS

The next country that you encounter as you drive south through Central America will be Honduras. It is the second-largest Central American country after Nicaragua and has a population of 5.5 million. The country is a land of many contrasts with with cool mountains in the interior and a long hot Caribbean coastline. Honduras is bordered by Guatemala on the West, the Caribbean on the North and Nicaragua, El Salvador and a tiny bit of the Pacific Ocean's Gulf of Fonesca on the South.

On his fourth voyage to the "new world" in 1502, Columbus landed near Trujillo on the Northern coast of Honduras. The name he gave it was "Honduras", which means "depths" in Spanish, referring to the deep waters of the Caribbean at that point.

The capital was established in Trujillo in 1525 by the Spanish. In 1537, the capital was moved to "Comayagua" in the much cooler highlands at near the geographical center of the country. It remained there until 1880, when it was once again moved. This time it was relocated to Tegucigalpa where it remains today.

By around 1600 the British pirates had just about taken over the **Bay Island**s off the North coast of Honduras. Henry Morgan established his headquarters on **Roatán**, the largest of the Bay Islands, which is a continuation of the barrier reef off Belize and Guatemala. English is the prime language in most of the Bay Islands, which consist of **Roatán**, **Guanaja** and **Utila**, the smaller of the group.

The most interesting section of Honduras from an archaeological point of view, is **Copán**, located west of San Pedro Sula near the Guatemalan border. The magnificient Copán Ruins, or sometimes just called Copán, are a sight to behold. The Mayans established and occupied the ruins for over 2000 years. They are now open from 8:00 a.m. to 4:00p.m. daily. There is a nominal entrance fee. The facilities contain a free audio visual show of the ruins. There is also a patio and restaurant loctaed in the facility. Outside there are restaurants and snack bars. Since this area has become a prime tourist attraction there is ample lodging and also places to eat in town.

Some of the sights one can expect to see are the **Great Plaza** with many carvings, the **Ball Court** which is the second largest in Central America, the **Hieroglyphic Stairway** with 63 steps with carvings which are thought to tell the history of Copán, stelae(an upright stone slab with inscriptions), the **Acropolis**, **Las Sepulturas**, and much more. Books and guides are available at the Visitor's Center. In the town of Copán, which is nearby, the **Museo de Copán** is filled with artifacts that were taken from the ruins.

SAN PEDRO SULA: This is the second-largest city in Honduras and has over 300,000 inhabitants. It is the commercial, business and industrial center of the country and main lay over for traveling to the north coast— about 40 miles away. As it is only 250 feet above sea-level and near the Caribbean, it is very hot and humid a lot of the time.

The city sadly lacks much in the way of sightseeing. This was partly due to its having suffered fire and flooding which wiped out its Colonial buildings of the early days. There are some parks and museums for your pleasure.

PUERTO CORTES, located north of San Pedro Sula, is Honduras' major port on the Caribbean. It is primarily a shipping point for most of the country's exports. Bananas and pineapple are the largest commodity. Being a commercial port, it has very little to offer for the tourist.

TELA is one of best beaches on Honduras' Caribbean coast and attracts many travellers. Accommodations are plentiful and inexpensive.

LA CEIBA which is the largest and busiest of Honduras' towns on the North Caribbean coast, is also a major shipping point for its exports. The area has nice beaches and is the closest port to Roatán and the Bay Islands.

THE BAY ISLANDS are famous for their warm Caribbean waters, coral reefs, white sand beaches, tropical sunsets and some of the best diving in the world. The islands are located about 30 miles off the north coast of Honduras.

Roatán is the largest and the most famous of the three Bay Islands. It is surrounded by about 60 miles of living reef, making it a paradise for diving and snorkelling. There is a lot to do to stay busy and hotels and restaurants are plentiful. You can even learn to dive if you have never tried it. The other two Bay Islands are **Guanaja** and **Utila**. The latter is the cheaper of the three islands to visit. Guanaja is the easternmost island and a good diving spot because of the reefs and sunken ships in the area. About 90% of the island has been declared a national forest and marine park.

TEGUCIGALPA is four hours (239 km) south of San Pedro Sula and is the capital city of Honduras. Around 800,000 inhabitants live in this city. It is located at an elevation of 3200 feet, is pleasantly cool, and surrounded by pine forests and several peaks. The weather is much cooler than on the coast making it better for living. The city is divided by the Choluteca River, with the main part of the city on the east side. On the other side of the river is a district called Comayaguele, which is a poor district with cheap hotels and is best to avoid.

Some of the sights in Tegucigalpa are **Parque Central** (Central Park), **La Merced** and the **Palacio Legislativo**, where congress meets, the **Casa Presidencial** which is the Presidential Palace.

The city has foreign embassies, plenty of hotels, all sorts of restaurants and nightlife, several English-language bookshops and even an English-language newspaper, *Honduras This Week*. Because of the cool weather and low cost of living, there is an expatriate community found in this city. We know several North Americans who moved from Costa Rica to Honduras because it is less expensive to live there.

If traveling to Nicaragua, Costa Rica or Panama, it is faster to travel through the lower western part of Honduras from El Salvador via Central American Highway 1(CA-1) and not visit either Tegucigalpa let alone San Pedro Sula on the other side of the country. There is no real need to go out of your way unless you want to visit either of these two large cities.

CHOLUTECA is a small city three hours (137 km) south of Tegucigalpa. There is not much in the way to do in this city. However, it is a main stopping-off point between borders and a good place to spend the night. It is only about 25 miles from the Nicaraguan border.

It is a good idea to cross that border as early in the day as possible. As with all border crossing, make sure you have all of your paperwork in order and be prepared for long waits and to exercise a lot of patience. Be aware that the Honduran border crossing is reputed to be the worst in Central America.

NICARAGUA ROUTE MAP

NICARAGUA

Nicaragua is the largest country in Central America, and has probably had the most tumultous history of all the Central American counties. The present population of the country is around 4,000,000 people. An archaeological site in the capital city of Managua has revealed evidence of civilization having existed here some 10,000 years ago. It appears that the population was buried in the ash of a volcano as the people were trying to flee its eruption.

The first contact Europeans had with Nicaraguans was when Columbus came to the Caribbean coast in 1502 on his fourth voyage. Later when the Spaniards came to Nicaragua in 1522, they followed the Río San Juan up to Lake Nicaragua, where they found the southern shores of the lake populated by Indians.

Much later during the California Gold Rush of 1848, the gold seekers wanted to find a quicker and safer way to reach California from the East. By sailing to San Juan del Norte, a sea-port on the Caribbean, which was the outlet of Río San Juan, they could go up this navigable river to Lake Nicaragua, then across the lake to the port of San Jorge. From there it was only about 20 km by stagecoach to the Pacific seaport of San Juan del Sur, where they boarded waiting ships on to California. The American tycoon Cornelius Vanderbilt operated the steamship company that carried passengers across Lake Nicaragua. Later, this route was considered very carefully as the route to build a canal across the isthmus. This canal was later built in Panama. Since then there have been rumors of several countries building a new canal across Nicaragua after the Panama Canal reverts back to Panamanian control at the end of this century.

One historical note of interest. In the mid-1850's an American by the name of Willim Walker with a small band of followers took over the government of Nicaragua and held power for over a year. His idea was to make Central America a colony of the U.S. He was later driven from power an eventually excuted.

In 1937 the infamous Somoza family came into power. The first of the Somozas was Anastasio Somoza Garcia Commander of the National Guard, who overthrew the elected government and took power as President. He amassed a great fortune and had land holdings larger than the country of El Salvador. It is said that he virtually owned the whole country. Anastio Somoza was assassinated in 1956, and was succeeded by his oldest son, Luis Somoza Debayle, who subsequently died in 1967. His younger brother, Anastio Somoza Debayle took over.

In 1974 the Sandinistas were founded in opposition to Somoza. Fighting continued until the Sandinistas won and marched triumphantly into Managua on July 19, 1979. The armed struggle continued all through the 1980s between the Sandinistas and the opposing Contras. In 1988, President Oscar Arias Sánchez of Costa Rica proposed the final peace plan that was signed by the Presidents of Costa Rica, El Salvador, Nicaragua, Guatemala and Honduras. For his work on this peace plan, Arias was awarded the Nobel Peace Prize.

Violeta Barrios de Chamorro was elected President in 1990, and peace was somewhat restored to this embattled nation. There have occasional flare-ups of sporadic violence from time to time, so is best to check for travel advisorys from the U.S. State Department before you decide to enter the country. However, we have never heard of any Americans being affected byNicaragua's politcal problems while travelling through the country by car.

The good news is that peace has virtually come to all of the regions former "hot spots". You shouldn't have any problems. The last country to end its civil war was Guatemala at the end of 1996. You should plan to follow the Pan-American Highway through this country , and only drive during day.

Like the other Central American countries, except El Salvador, and Belize, Nicaragua stretches from the Caribbean side to the Pacific Ocean. The country three distinct different regions:

THE CARIBBEAN REGION is characterized by a wide coastal plain and is the largest in Central America, averaging 50 miles in width. It has many rivers and lagoons with dense tropical rain forests, and is sparsely populated.

THE NORTH CENTRAL REGION is composed of the high mountains and valleys which are more sparsely populated than the coastal areas, but supplies about one quarter of the agriculture products of the country. The highest point in Nicaragua—**Pico Mogotón** (6898 feet) is in this area.

THE PACIFIC COAST REGION is a low-land plain that is hot, fertile and stretches along the Pacific Coast. This area contains several volcanoes. Some of them are **San Cristóbal**(5724 feet), **Concepión** (5281 feet), **Momotombo** (4198 feet) and **Masaya** or **Santiago** (4471 feet). **Lake Nicaragua** is the largest lake in Central America and has the only fresh water sharks in the world. They were cut off from the ocean in ancient times when the lake became landlocked after an earthquake.

MANAGUA with a population of almost one million is the capital of Nicaragua. Located on the shore of **Lake Managua,** the city is less than 200 feet above sea level, so it has an average daytime temperature of 88 degrees. Over twenty-five percent of the population of the country lives in Managua. The center of the city was vritually destroyed by the earthquake of 1976 and further damaged during the revolution of 1978-79. There are some notable old buildings and a couple of museums. Boats can be hired to visit the still-smoking **Momotombo** volcano on the shore of Lake Managua, west of the city near León. There are several resorts on the Pacific side about an hour's driving time from Managua. They are **Pochomil**, **Masachapa**, **Cesares** and **La Boquita**.

LEON is located northwest of the city of Managua. It was founded in 1524 and is one of the oldest cities in Nicaragua. It is located on the shore of Lake Managua at the foot of the Moomotombo volcano. Eruptions from the volcano have damaged the city several times, the latest being in 1992.

GRANADA is Nicaragua's oldest city and the country's third city of importance. It was built by the Spaniards in 1523 on the shores of Lake Nicaragua at the foot of **Mombacho** volcano. Much of the old city was burned to the ground by William Walker in 1856. This city has always had access to the Caribbean via Lake Nicaragua and the Río San Juan, and originally became the principal trading city with Europe. It has many interesting old Spanish buildings.

LAKE NICARAGUA is the largest lake in Central America. It has many islands which you can visit by boat. The **Isla de Ometepec** is a double island with two volcanoes—**Volcano Concepción** (5281 feet), and **Volcano Madera** (4395 feet). Mt. Conception last erupted in 1983.

RIVAS is the last city of importance on the Pan-American Highway or CA-1 before leaving Nicaragua to enter Costa Rica. Again, be sure to have all of your papers in order before you cross the border at Peñas Blancas.

COSTA RICA ROUTE MAP

COSTA RICA

Costa Rica is the third smallest Central American country and lies between Nicaragua on the north and Panama on the south. The country has just over 3 million inhabitants with Panama and Belize only having less. The country is unique in that it has the highest percentage of people of European ancestry in Cental America and almost no peolple of Indian descent.

When Columbus made his fourth voyage to the new world in 1502, he landed in what is now, Costa Rica. In the hope of finding such treasures as silver and gold, he named this country "Costa Rica", which translates into "Rich Coast". His wishes of finding the precious metals did not materialize. However, he did find a country that has become fabulously rich in other resources.

In the years that followed Columbus' trip, Europeans—mostly Spaniards—settled into this "paradise". The climate along the Caribbean coast is hot and humid with an average temperature of 85 degrees, and with its tropical rains, has become one of the main banana producing areas of Central America.

Around 60 percent of the European settlers came to the Central Highlands, because of the excellent year-round spring-like weather. The average temperature in the Central Valley is a pleasant 74 degrees. San José is the modern capital of Costa Rica and has grown into the largest city in the country with a population of just over one million in the metropolitan area. It remains quaintly charming despite being the most cosmopolitan city in Central America.

The Pacific Coast of Costa Rica has warm temperatures with an average of 84 degrees. Guanacaste province is hot and dry. The country also has numerous rain forests. There is lush tropical vegetation along both coasts with hundreds of miles of white and dark sand beaches. Puntarenas province, the largest province in Costa Rica, occupies about two thirds of the Pacific Coast.

Much of the country's topography reminds one of Switzerland's rugged forest-covered mountains with cattle grazing in lush pastures. Furthermore, much like the Swiss, the Costa Ricans developed a peaceful democracy with no army. The "ticos", as the people are called, are an extremely friendly race who have constantly striven for as perfect a social and political environment as possible. They have the highest per capita income, largest middle class and standard of living of all the countries in Central America. Furthermore,they have achieved an impressive 93 percent literacy rate, a higher longevity rate than the U.S. (76.3 vs. 76) and enjoy universal medical coverage that frees the mind of the worries that plague so many other countries of the world.

These ambitious, family loving people take extreme pride in their National Park System, which has been developed to encompass 12 percent of the territory of the country. It shelters over 12,000 varieties of plants, nearly 250 species of mammals, some 850 different kinds of birds and over 350 different reptiles and amphibians. Geologists and biologists are still trying to catalogue all of the different species of birds, animals, insects and butterflies that inhabit the rain forest canopies as well as the waters and coral reefs that are found in Costa Rica and many islands along its coasts.

All of this and more are found in this "paradise" which is about the size of West Virginia, and lying just ten degrees north of the equator. Is it no wonder that vacationers and immigrants are flocking to this country in ever increasing numbers.

Costa Ricans have been nominated twice for the Nobel Peace Prize. In 1987, President Oscar Arias Sánchez was awarded the Nobel Peace Prize—a great achievement for such a small country. Arias is still striving to convince the neighboring countries to follow his lead, and to "turn their swords into plowshares." His strategy has worked because there are no more civil wars or guerilla movements operating in any of the former strife-torn nations like Nicaragua, El Salvador or Guatemala. Costa Rica's United Nation Peace University has an outstanding curriculum for those graduate students seeking their Masters Degrees. Just to name the achievements of this wonderful country makes one feel he or she is bragging. Costa Rica seems too good to be true.

ENTRANCE REQUIREMENTS

The requirements for entering the country are simple. Citizens of the United States and Canada are cleared at the airports or border check points with their passports. Visas and mandatory car insurance (for those driving) are issued at the border upon entering the country. Additional car insurance may be purchased from I.N.S., the government insurance agency. Check with the Costa Rican consulate or the Costa Rican National Tourist Office for additional information.,

The official language of Costa Rica is Spanish. English is being taught in the schools almost to the point of becoming a second language. There are presently two major weekly English language newspapers. There is the well-established *Tico Times* and the newer *Costa Rica Today*. The *Tico Times* is more "newsy", and has very good regular columns on such topics as health, gardening, sightseeing and other points of interest. *Costa Rica Today* goes more into articles on Costa Rican history, sightseeing and other points of interest. You may find yourself getting both papers for their guidance and calendars of local events.

In addition to the newspapers, there are several booklet type publications that are available, covering different points of interest. If you are planning to come to Costa Rica you might do well to obtain some of these books, as each covers a different area in depth. Of course, there is this book if you intend to drive to Central America. For reading about travelling around Costa Rica in depth and sightseeing, etc., we strongly recommend *The New Key To Costa Rica*. You may purchase this book at most bookstores in the Costa Rica or through: **Publications In English**, APDO 7-1230, 1000 San Jose, Costa Rica. It can also be found in almost every large bookstore in the U.S. and Canada. Moon Publication's, *Costa Rica Handbook* is an excellent guide. Another book to have for all of Central America which we mentioned earlier is *Central America On A Shoestring*. See the "Suggested Reading " section at the end of this book for more titles.

Since Costa Rica has so much to offer foreigners and is so Americanized, it is no wonder it has the largest expatriate community in Central America. More North Americans per capita live in Costa Rica than any other country in the world. Around 20,000 at last count. Many are retireees and others are just people tired of the "rat race" seeking alternative lifestyles. In Costa Rica there is something for everyone and everything for someone. If you are planning to retire, you may want to get the best-selling guidebook, *The Golden Door to Retirement and Living in Costa Rica* by our publisher, Costa Rica Books, Suite 1 SJO 981, P.O. Box 025216, Miami, FL 33102-5216 or call 800-365-2342 (Please the ad on page 4 in Chapter 1 for more details).

VOLCANOES

There are numerous volcanoes in Costa Rica. Some are still active to a small degree, while others have been dormant for many years. The more popular ones to visit and that are easily accessible are:

POAS VOLCANO NATIONAL PARK (9,000 ft. above sea level) is easily accessible from either Heredia or Alajuela, with good paved roads right into the park. There is an easy walking trail from the parking lot to the viewing area, which is only about 200 yards. There is also an information center, snack stands, restrooms, and picnic and barbecue areas. From the viewing area one can see the smoking, boiling lava in a lake in its crater. One should plan to visit it in the early morning before the clouds form and spoil your view.

IRAZU VOLCANO: (11,257 + ft.) is the highest of the Costa Rica's volcanoes, is easily accessible by car or bus, and is just north of Cartago, the former capital of Costa Rica. It affords one a spectacular view of the surrounding area, as well as both the Caribbean and the Pacific on a clear day. It last erupted in 1963, and now has five dormant craters. It is best to get there very early in the morning before the clouds form. Facilities include an Information Center, restrooms, and hiking trails.

ARENAL VOLCANO: (5,356 ft.) is a very active volcano that exploded in 1968, killing quite a number of people with its lava flows. The nearest town to it is Fortuna, six kilometers to the west. At nighttime one can get spectacular views of the red-hot lava and rocks flying through the air. This volcano is more of what most people think that a volcano should be—a perfect cone-shaped mountain.

BARVA VOLCANO: (9,531 ft.) Located in "Braulio Carrillo National Park" about five km above San José de la Montaña. They scenry while you drive up the mountain is spectacular. This area looks much like Switzerland with its many pine trees and alpine-like pastures except there is no snow. You can park your car in Sacramento and take the trail to the volcano (about 9 km). There you will see several lakes and numerous waterfalls. It is also one of the best places in Costa Rica to see the *Quetzales* which are one of the most beautiful birds in the world. You are supposed to have good luck if you view one of these remarkable birds. The best time to make this trip is during the dry season, from December to April. Camping is permitted, and there is plenty of good water in the streams and waterfalls which abound.

NATIONAL PARKS & SANCTUARIES

As stated before, about 12 percent of Costa Rica has been set aside for national parks and sanctuaries. Weekends will find the parks teeming with Tico families, who like to do their outings as a family unit on Sundays. You may wish to avoid the crowds and plan your excursion on the weekdays. Some of the Parks are:

BRAULIO CARRILLO NATIONAL PARK: One of the greatest engineering feats in this country was when the highway was built through Braulio Carrillo National Park on the route from San José to Limón. It was feared that such a road would ruin the park. It has proven to be an asset, as it has brought the local residents closer to nature. Careful planning has opened up this rain forest for public viewing, without harm to nature. There are a few hiking trails from roadside parks into the forest. One should be prepared, however, as the trails are usually muddy, slick and steep. There is an entrance with good hiking trails above San José de la Montaña. (See Barva Volcano above). Braulio Carrillo Park is not only very large, but it ranges in elevation from the top of Barva Volcano, 9,531 feet to a low in the Caribbean lowlands of only 164 feet, giving it a wide range of birds, animals and plants.

CAHUITA NATIONAL PARK: This Park is on the Caribbean, south of Limón, and is noted for its snorkeling and beautiful coral reef. There is also a jungle near the camp ground at Puerto Vargas where one may see iguanas, sloths and monkeys.

CHIRRIPO NATIONAL PARK: This Park is reached from San Isidro on the southern Pacific side in the center of the country. Cerro Chirripó peak is 12,526 feet high—the highest point in Costa Rica. There are hiking trails and mountain huts—all above 6,500 feet elevation. Be prepared for low temperatures at night. It is best to come to this Park during the dry season at mid-week, as the park is crowded on the weekends. Carry your own water.

CORCOVADO NATIONAL PARK: Located on the southwest tip of the Osa Peninsula in the southwestern corner of Costa Rica. It is home to the scarlet macaws along with some 400 species of birds including the near-extinct harpy eagle. Also protected here are tapirs, giant anteaters, sloths, monkeys, crocodiles and five species of the cat family. Basic accommodations are available at the main ranger station at Sirena, but one must book in advance. It is best to visit this Park during the dry season.

GUANACASTE NATIONAL PARK: This is a new national park, built in conjunction with the Santa Rosa National Park, the two being separated by the Pan-American Highway. It was built to allow the wildlife of Santa Rosa to migrate to the higher mountains of Orosi Volcano (4,867 ft.) and Cacao Volcano (5,441 ft.). Of note are the massive numbers of moths that breed in the high, dry climate of the volcanoes, then return to the lower, warmer Santa Rosa Park. It is estimated that over 3,800 species of moths inhabit this area. In addition, there are wild pigs in the area. Biological stations in the park can accommodate up to 40 people in dormitories in rooms with cold water, or one may camp in assigned areas.

SANTA ROSA NATIONAL PARK: This park is between the city of Liberia and the Costa Rica-Nicaraguan border. You must pay an entrance fee at the park entrance. Maps of the park are also sold there and there is camping. The campground has drinking water, picnic tables, cold showers and flush toilets. Meals are available at the ranger headquarters, and horse rentals are inexpensive. If you keep your eyes open on the trails, you may see monkeys, iguanas, snakes and other animals. Along the beaches, one may see several thousand Olive Ridley Turtles at one time during their nesting season form September to October.

GUAYABO NATIONAL MONUMENT: This is the most noted archaeological site in the country. It was inhabited from around 1000 B.C. to 1400 A.D. There were an estimated 10,000 inhabitants in the area. It is not known why they disappeared before the Spaniards arrived in the country. About 10 percent of the monument is an excavated area. The remainder is rain forest. The ruins are open from 8 a.m. to 4 p.m. on weekends and holidays. It is closed during the week. Camping is permitted and there are toilets, drinking water and a picnic area.

MANUEL ANTONIO NATIONAL PARK: It is the smallest but most popular park in the system. It is located a few miles south of the town of Quepos. To enter the park one must walk on the trails and wade across an estuary at the park entrance. The water is about four feet deep during high tide, so it starts out as an experience. The trails lead to three beaches and an over-looking cliff with great views. One is almost sure to see monkeys during the day on the park trails, as well as sloths, armadillos, racoons, peccaries, coatimundis, snakes, lizards iguanas and other animals. There are a reported 350 kinds of birds in the park. Carry your own water and sun screen. The park closes at 4 p.m. and there is no camping allowed in the park. The Manuel Antonio Park probably has the one of most beautiful coastline in the entire world.

MONTEVERDE CLOUD FOREST PRESERVE: This is a place where you must spend more than one day to see everything the area has to offer. You can pick up maps, trail guides and other information at the entrance. The road into the reserve takes about two hours, and is rough, steep and dusty in the dry season. During the rainy season you will need a four-wheel vehicle to reach this area. You should also have rain gear if you plan to do any hiking during this time of year.

The Tropical Science Center who operates the preserve wishes to keep it that way. The entrance is open from 7 a.m. to 4 p.m. daily and they charge $5.00 per day or $29.50 per week. Accommodations range from $3.00 for a bunk to deluxe accommodations in some of the hotels located in Santa Elena, 3 km from Monteverde. There are also camping facilities available. There are guides available to take you on a tour—the best way to see all there is to see—which you might miss if you are on your own.

OSTIONAL NATIONAL WILDLIFE REFUGE: This refuge is only about four miles long and just a few hundred yards wide. Its main purpose is to protect the nesting area of the Olive Ridley Sea Turtle. Nesting or *La arribada* takes place from April to December, with the most activity in August and September. The people are allowed to harvest the eggs the first 36 hours of the laying season, but guards prevent further taking of eggs after that time. There are cabins and a couple of hotels are available. Meals may be purchased from local residents.

TORTUGUERO NATIONAL PARK: The area north of Limón is noted for being the largest nesting area in the Caribbean for the Green Sea Turtle. To get to there, one must take a tour, or hire a boat, as there are no roads to the park. In 1974, a series of canals were built so the city of Tortuguero would have an inland waterway connection. Tortuguero National Park's beaches are the largest in the Caribbean where the Green Sea Turtles come to lay their eggs. Their nesting season is from July through September. Visitors may watch the turtles lay their eggs, as well view the baby turtles hatch. In addition to watching the turtles, Tortuguero has many other interesting things to see. By trail or boat trips, one can view various kinds of monkeys, sloths and dozens of other jungle animals, hundreds of different kinds of birds, lizards and other water creatures.

PANAMA ROUTE MAP

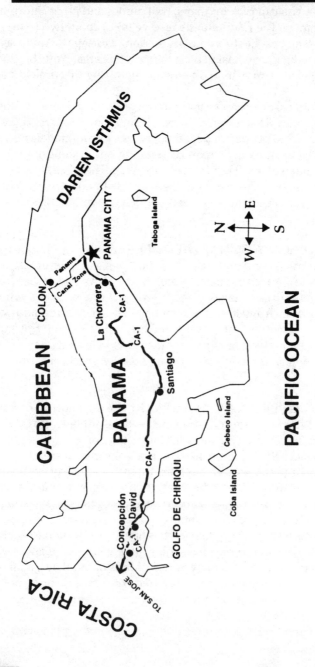

PANAMA

Panama is situated at the Southern end of Central America —between Costa Rica to the west, Colombia to the east, the Caribbean to the north and the Pacific Ocean to the south. The country is divided almost equally by the Panama Canal, which starts from the Pacific near Panama City and goes Northwest to the Caribbean, at the City of Colón, just some 50 miles distance.

Panama has about 2.5 million people most of who live in the two largest cities. Most of the people are *mestizos* or mixed with a 15% black and a small Indian population. Just as in the rest of Central America, the country has both a rainy and dry season. The climate is hot at lower elevations and gets cooler the higher you climb. Panama City tends to be very hot and very humid because of its low elevation.

The Pan-American Highway presently ends in the jungles of Darien near the Colombian border at a place called Yaviza. Those wishing to continue their drive into South America must take an auto ferry from Panama to Colombia, where they pick up the Pan-American Highway to the southern tip of South America. Maybe some day the final stretch of the Pan-American Highway will be built linking North, Central and South America. If this ever happens, it will be possible to make a trip by car from Alaska to the tip of South America.

Of course one cannot visit Panama without seeing the Panama Canal. Its numerous locks moving huge tankers and massive cruise ships are a sight to behold. There is also the 50-mile Isthmus Railroad from which you may view the ships moving from one ocean to the other through the canal.

The idea to build a canal across the Isthmus of Panama was first proposed in the 1500s. The French were the first to undertake this monumental project in the late 1800s. However, a combination of yellow fever, malaria and money problems forced them to halt construction. In 1903 Panama, backed by the U.S., declared its independence from Colombia. Shortly afterwards the U.S. signed a treaty with Panama giving it soverign rights over the Canal Zone.

The U.S. started construction in 1904. The project became one of the greatest engineering feats of the 20th century. Yellow fever and malaria were virtually eliminated enabling the 75,000 workers to finish this project in ten years. The first ship sailed through the canal on on August 15, 1914. Over the years U.S. control of the canal proved to be a source of constant friction with Panama.

A new treaty was signed in 1977 promising to give Panama full control. The canal zone is gradually being incorporated into Panamanian juristiction. This process will end in the year 2000, when Panama takes over operation of the canal. Also, the U.S. milarity presence is to gradually be phased out according to the most recent treaty. The U.S. has played an important role in Panamain history since the country gained its independence from Colombia.

In 1988 the U.S. carried out "Operation Just Cause" to remove the Panamain dictator, Manuel Noriega from power. Noriga has amassed power and became involved in drug trafficking. He also murdered some of his opponents and rigged elections. When he began to become involved with the Colombian drug cartels the U.S. indicted him for drug trafficking and money laundering. Then when he nullified a democratic election victory by the oppostion, the U.S. had no choice but to invade.

By the way, the main unit of currency is the U.S. dollar. The only other country in Latin America to use the U.S. dollar as the main unit of currency is Puerto Rico.

The original residents of Panama were the Kuna Indians of the San Blas Archipelago, located on the northeast shores of Panama. They occupied this area in pre-Columbian times. On this coast made up of several hundred small islands, the Kunas still live, making their colorful, intricately layered blouses. Each of these blouses is a work of art.

To the South of San Blas in the Darien jungles, are the Choco Indians who still carry on the life-style of bygone centuries. They live in thatched roof shelters, cook over open fires and sleep in hammocks. They are a people who live deep in the jungles where the Pan-American Highway ends.

At the far West end of Panama in the mountains near the Costa Rican border, the Guaymi Indians live with their colorful costumes and their authentic handcrafted collars called *"chaquiras"*. In this area of the mountains of Chiriqui Province are the best known peaks. The highest one, **Cerro Punta** and the **Baru Volcano**, which has been dormant for several hundreds of years. This part of the country is noted for its cool mountain trails for hikers, abundant trout streams for the anglers and horseback riding. It is a "bird-watchers paradise" as well as for those interested in the many gorgeous plants that abound in the forests.

About two hours by car from Panama City is **El Valle**, noted for its "square trees" and the "golden toads", whose skin gleams like sunshine.

For the die-hard fisherman, the waters of Panama teem with record-setting sailfish, tuna, black and blue marlin. Charterboat captains will take you where you can try to set a new world record.

Columbus made a landing on his fourth voyage at Portobello, which was named for the beautiful port that it was. It was from this port that the riches that were taken from the Incas of Peru, were shipped by Spanish galleons to Spain. These fabled riches naturally attracted such seamen as Sir Frances Drake. The area now called Panama also attracted famous pirates such as Henry Morgan, who at one time, plundered an entire year's collection of Spanish gold that had been taken by the Spaniards from the Incas in Peru. This act encouraged Morgan to greater feats. In 1671 he came with 37 galleons and with over 2000 men, sacked and captured old Panama City. The old forts still stand at Portobelo for you to visit when you walk through the ruins of old Panama.

PANAMA CITY, is the capital of the country and has a population of about 600,000. It is a modern cosmopolitan city and one of the world's foremost international banking, business and trade centers. The city has branches of more than 150 banks from around the world. Panama like Switzerland is famous for its "bank secrecy" and "off-shore" corporations. Skyscrapers dot the city's skyline and first-class hotels abound. Entertainment and nightline are excellent. There are always top performers to entertain you, whether you are on vacation or there for business. The city's convention faclities can handle 10,000 visitors at a time.

Panama City is also noted for its duty-free shops for your shopping pleasure. A large selection of first-rate restaurants abound. You have your choice of French, Japanese, Peruvian, Chinese, Italian, Mexican, Swiss, or Spanish. There are also MacDonald's, Burger King or Kentucky Fried Chicken where you can grab a bite on the run. You may also gamble at one of the many casinos, where all of your winnings are TAX FREE!

The Spanish moved Panama City to its present location, and rebuilt it into a place of old-world charm. You may walk through the cobblestone streets and visit such historical places as museums, galleries, the National Theatre, the old convent that holds the rare "flat arch", "*Las Bovedas*" the old Spanish jail, and the church whose entire altar is layered with gold.

Even if you are not planning a trip through the canal you can vist the nearby Miraflores Locks. A bilingual guide will explain how they operate.

There are also a few good beaches you can visit near Panama City.. Check out **Kobbe**, **Veracruz**, **San Carlo**s and **Playa El Palmar** beaches.

Another enchanting day can be experienced by taking a cruise from near the Pacific entrance to the canal to the island of **Tobogo** located about 14 miles off the coast. It is also known as"Isle of Flowers". There is an interesting fishermen's village where you may dine or just enjoy the sandy beach.

There is also nearby **Contadora Island**, with its resort hotels, casino, swimming pools, lighted tennis courts, diving, snorkeling, windsurfing and golf.

COLON is a city of 60,00 located at the Caribbean entrance to the canal and Panama's second largest city. It has the world's second largest duty-free port after Hong Kong. It is a dangerous city because of the rampant crime. There is no real reason to visit this city.

DRIVING TO PANAMA: There are three border crossing on the border between Costa Rica and Panama. Paso Canoas, located along the Pan-American Highway (CA-1), is the place you will most likely cross the border from Costa Rica to Panama. The border crossing at Paso Canoas opens at 7 am and closes at 10 pm . David is the first city of importance after you cross the border and Panam's third-largest city. Since the drive from San José, Costa Rica to Panama City takes over 10 hours you may want to spend the night in David. A large number of travellers stop there overnight on there way to and from the Costa Rica border about 35 miles away. There are a number of places to stay and a surprising array of reataurants where you can dine. The Pan-American Highway is much better in Panama than in southern Costa Rica, so you should make better driving time.

CHAPTER IV

ACTUAL TRIP ALONG THE PAN-AMERICAN HIGHWAY

This chapter recounts the author's trip from California to Costa Rica on the Pan-American Highway. The next chapter contains stories of other people's trips which they submitted to us.
This includes driving in recreation vehicles, as well as a trip pulling a trailer.

While you are making your trip, keep a log or notes of everything that happened to you such as road conditions, your routes, experiences at border crossings, hotels and motels where you stayed and anything else that may help someone who is planning to make this trip in the future. This way we can include your accounts and any significant changes in forthcoming editions of this guidebook. Please send all information to:

COSTA RICA BOOKS
Suite 1 SJO 981
P.O. BOX 025216
Miami, FL 33102-5216
Fax: 619-4216002 U.S. or 011-506-232-5613

AUTHOR'S TRIP - CALIFORNIA
TO COSTA RICA

So that you may have an idea of what to expect on a drive on the Pan-American Highway, the following is a day-by-day account of our drive from El Toro, California to San José de la Montaña, Costa Rica. You will realize that just about any one can make the trip. I was 73 years of age, and my wife was 59. She had been a stewardess with both American Airlines on the Dallas to Mexico City run, and with TACA Airlines throughout Central America. She had taken Spanish in High School, and her flight career had given her sufficient background that, with the help of her English-Spanish dictionary, she was able to handle most situations we would encounter. My Spanish was limited to the four-letter words boys learn, and which were of no help in this situation.

In case you do not speak Spanish—Don't worry! You will have no problem finding someone who speaks *"poquito"* English. With the aid of your Spanish English dictionary (which is a "must"), you look up key words in English, and let them read the Spanish translation, and you will get by. I understand that you can now buy an English-Spanish pocket calculator where you spell the word in English, and the calculator gives you the Spanish word for it. To assist you, we have included some key phrases so you can get your idea across and make yourself understood. When using this method of dialogue, do not memorize the Spanish phrase and try them out, or you will end up with a five-minute response that will blow your mind. My wife says that she is afraid to ask a question, because they might answer. (Also see the handy Spanish survival book and cassette we advertise in this book).

If you do speak high school level Spanish, do not be afraid to ask people to speak slowly, or they will rattle it off like a machine gun. Actually you will find this a fun game, making yourself understood. When it comes to numbers, I either hand them a pen and paper so they can write the numbers, or just hand them a pocket calculator (which is also a "must") and just let them punch out the numbers for you.

Once we had made all of the preparations listed in the first chapter, we were ready to make our trip. As we wanted to stay away from as much hot weather as possible, and because the AAA book had hinted of possible problems on the west coast route, we decided to stick to the route that followed the higher altitudes, and had more larger cities.

That would mean that we would enter Mexico via Laredo, Texas. As I have a son and grandchildren living in Killeen, Texas, this was an added advantage for an en route visit.

I will skip the California to Texas drive, except to mention that it did give us a chance to discover a couple of mechanical problems with the car that we were able to fix before entering Mexico.

We were driving a seven-year-old Plymouth Voyager mini-van with four cylinders. We felt it was in good enough shape to endure the trip with no problem after we had it checked out and serviced. We had removed the rear seats and shipped them to Costa Rica with our furniture. We rigged up the springs of a twin bed with plywood panels to serve as legs on each end, and to hold the springs at sufficient height to allow storage of some boxes filled with items we would need until our furniture arrived in Costa Rica. We put a new mattress on the bed, along with making it up with sheets, blankets and pillows. Just before we left El Toro, some sweet person gave us a feather comforter that added a touch of luxury. If we got tired enroute, we had a place for a nap.

We also included an ice chest for en route snacks. It was a Coleman-type, which I strongly recommend. The most important—and useful item that is absolutely a "must", was a folding porta-potty.

After a nice visit with the family and grandchildren, we left Killeen early in the morning of January 22nd, skirted San Antonio and arrived in Laredo in time for lunch. After servicing the car, we headed for the border.

The border guard, assuming we were just going to Nueva Laredo for shopping, waved us through. I told him that we were driving through Mexico, so he had us pull over and checked our papers. We had everything except the clearance for the car. He had a young soldier get into the car with us, who directed us a few blocks to an official compound. He told us to take our papers, the car registration, drivers license and passports, inside for clearance.

They pulled certain papers and had us take them to a clerk, where we paid one dollar for her to photocopy them. They made out some forms and punched some holes in a windshield sticker to indicate the valid dates, then went out to the car to verify that the car we were driving matched our paperwork. They put the sticker on the windshield and pointed us on the road out of town. They wished us *"Vaya con Diós"*, and after 1 1/2 hours, we were on our way south.

The first 25 miles were great. We were on a newly paved four lane divided highway where our speed averaged between 65 and 75 miles per hour. Then we came to a customs check point. They checked our passports, glanced at the back of the van, and waved us ahead, telling us what sounded like, *"directo"*. As we left the check point, we noticed that they were checking the luggage of the car that had left the compound while they were putting the sticker on our car.

After leaving the customs check, we found ourselves on a two lane road filled with chuck holes. So, for the next 50 or 60 miles we were lucky if we averaged 20 m.p.h..

In addition to the bad road conditions, the road was filled with slow moving trucks and buses. We soon learned that the truck and bus drivers throughout Mexico are very courteous. As soon as the road clears to where we could pass them, they signal with their left-turn indicators. If they are not moving into the passing lane, this meant for us to pass them. We missed a few opportunities to pass before we caught on to their method of signaling. Do it with caution, however, because they use the same turn indicators when they are going to pass a vehicle. The only difference is that when they are passing, they make their move at the same time they start signaling. Just use caution.

MONTERREY, MEXICO

We had crawled along the pothole-filled road for over two hours and noticed that there was a lot of construction to the left of the road. We suddenly came upon a brand new divided four-lane toll road. We knew this wider road would link with the divided four lane highway out of Nuevo Laredo, and that the drive to Monterrey would be a pleasure. By the time we arrived in Monterrey, we had gone through two toll plazas, and had paid a total of 33,000 pesos ($11.00) in tolls. (As of February 1997 there are 7.8 "New" pesos per dollar).

NOTE: The new monetary unit is called the " New Peso " or (N$). The value of the New Peso is equivalent to 1,000 old pesos. Since the rate of this floating currency is subject to daily fluctuatuions, we suggest you check to see actual exchange rate.

We arrived in Monterrey just as the sun was setting over the rugged mountains that surround the city. It was a beautiful sight, and we were extremely happy to have completed our first day in Mexico, with not one of those horrible things happening to us that our family and friends had warned us about.

We had intended to stay in one of those hotels listed in the AAA guide book. It was listed at $30.00, but as we were entering the main street of Monterrey, we came upon a very clean looking motel. We did a quick return and went back to check it out. The desk clerk showed me one of the rooms, and one could hardly ask for anything more adequate. It had two double beds, a clean bath and shower, and a little area with a table and two chairs. Then he told me the price was 33,000 pesos ($11.00), I whipped out my travellers checks to pay him.

Unfortunately, Karl Malden had not done a good job down here, because the motel would not accept them. In case you have never heard of Karl Malden, he is the actor who advertised American Express Travelers checks for many years on TV, claiming they could be cashed at any location in the world without a problem. He was so wrong.

As we needed gas for the following day, we decided to go the Pemex station (government owned gas stations) down the street, pay with a travelers check, then come back and pay for the motel out of our change. The only problem was that Karl had not done a selling job with Pemex. They would not accept our travellers checks, either.

A four-lane stretch of the Pan-American near San José, Costa Rica.

As we had originally planned to stay in the AAA $30.00 a night hotel, we decided we would have to blow the extra $20.00 we would have saved by staying at the motel, and go to the AAA hotel. It was a beautiful hotel, but there was a problem here, also. The rate listed in the AAA book was not $30.00—it had gone to $75.00. Ouch!

We did a quick count of our cash. We had $15.00 and change in U.S. currency between us. So it was back to the Autopista Motel. We paid the clerk the $11.00 in U.S. cash, which he gladly accepted. We were able to park right next to our door, so we took advantage of this to repack some of our luggage so that we each had just one suitcase and a box of needed items for each night in the future. We also brought in the ice chest and fixed our dinner from the contents. A real inexpensive first night in Mexico.

Early the next morning we packed up and drove a few blocks down the street to the Holiday Inn, which was as nice a hotel as any in the States. We had a hearty breakfast and paid the well-under $10.00 check with a $50.00 travellers check. Then we went to the hotel cashier and cashed another $100.00—so we were set for the day. We had our confidence in Karl Malden restored somewhat. One out of three tries were successful.

Our next stop was the "green" Pemex station, where we filled up with MAGNA SIN (unleaded supreme gas carried by only the green Pemex stations —in the green pump). As we left Monterrey, we noticed that it was quite an industrial city. Unfortunately, their cars emit a lot of black exhaust fumes, and there are lots of cars. The result is a layer of smog, even more dense than Los Angeles, that hangs over the area, held in by the ring of mountains that surround the city.

The mountains are beautiful, with great blocks of solid rock forming giant pinnacles, lined up along the mountain tops, looking like columns of soldiers marching off to war. The early morning sun glistened off their tops—or helmets—however your imagination sees them.

We left Monterrey on highway 40, but just short of Saltillo (about 50 miles), we turned south on Highway 57. This was a very good two-lane highway, and very fast except for the frequent back-up of cars caused by of trucks and busses. It was straight and open enough that we had no trouble passing,until mid-morning.

BREAKDOWN EN ROUTE

The car had been running like a clock until mid-morning. Then every time I would try to accelerate to pass a truck or bus, my engine would cut out like we were running out of gas. My gas gauge showed that I had plenty, so it had to be either the carburetor or a plugged gas line. My speed was slowed down considerably. I could see by the map that we would be coming to a sizable town in just a few miles. There were always Pemex stations in the larger towns, so all I had to do was get there. So long as I did not try to go too fast, it just seemed to plug along, but at a constantly slower speed.

We finally came to a town called Matehuala, which is about 200 miles south of Monterrey. We pulled into a Pemex station at the near edge of town, but they had no mechanic. They told me to go see a guy called "Madino" in town. In trying to find him, we came to a large automobile agency, so we pulled into their garage. Again, they told us to see Madino. They indicated that he was right up the street we were on. We drove to the end of the street, but could see anything that indicated "Madino". We pulled into another small gas station on a street corner about midtown. I was trying to find someone to ask when suddenly I saw a little single car garage on the side street with the name "Madino" above the door. I drove over and parked next to his driveway and found a young man in his mid-twenties inside. He verified his name was "Madino".

With Audrey's assistance we explained to him what the car had been doing. He took the car for a test drive with Audrey along to answer any questions. In 10 minutes they returned. He raised the hood and started taking the gas lines apart. He would blow on a line and his partner would listen in the gas tank. Satisfied with their findings, he took the gas filter off. He did not have a Plymouth filter, but came out with a "universal" filter which he replaced after modifying the gas line. When he had it replaced, he got back in the car for another test drive. In a few minutes he returned completely satisfied with his work. He charged me $25.00. I was happy, and so was he.

If you happen to be having a problem with your car and you are near Matehuala, I strongly recommend Hugo Madino for the job.

ON TO SAN LUIS POTOSI

So after a two hour mechanical delay, we hit the road again. Just a couple of miles south of Matehuala we came to a road sign that interested me very much. It read, "Tropic of Cancer - 23 Degrees 20 Minutes North Lattitude". That is the point over which the sun travels farthest north on June 20 - 21st of every year, and is the official start of summer in the Northern Hemisphere. At noon on that date, your shadow will be directly under you at that point. Also, as you drive south, your shadow will he south of you on that date. In the United States your shadow always falls to the north of you.

By this time it had started to rain, and we were in the rain until early the next morning. As we drove along this very good road, we noticed there were little road-side shelters made with four poles, one at each corner, about three or four feet high, that held the roof. Covering the tops of each shelter was cardboard, plastic or sometimes a piece of corrugated iron to keep the rain off of the one to four occupants huddled together. To protect them from the blustery winds, was sometimes more cardboard, a piece of cloth, a piece of plastic, some twigs woven together, and sometimes, nothing at all. They usually had a small fire burning right in front, and they would be crowded together for warmth.

Strung along the roadside in front of their shelters were different kinds of wares for sale. Some pottery, many snake skins, and even a small bird cage made from twigs or bamboo, with some sort of birds in them. All of this was in an area of no trees and with only scrub brush to gather for their fires.

The vegetation in this area was very desert-like, with tall plants that resembled the "yucca" plants of the Mojave Desert of California.

A very interesting thing that we noticed for the first time in this area, was the fences that were around the little mud-adobe houses alongside of the road. They were made of straight post-shaped cactus about three or four feet tall, planted right up against each other to form a solid barrier of sharp thorns. I could see where they would turn away any potential intruder.

Another thing we saw throughout Mexico, was what appeared to be small graves or shrines along the roadside. Some were very simple not big enough to be a grave as one sees in a cemetery. Others were simple crosses, while still others were elaborate mausoleum-type structures not more than a foot or two square. A few had the replica of Christ, while others had a replica of Mother Mary inside. They were all visible from the road. In one instance there were six of these little "graves" side by side, alongside the road. We wondered if they were perhaps, a memorial for people who were killed along the road. Later, this was confirmed that it was, indeed, a memorial for that reason.

It was about 5:00 p.m. when we arrived in San Luis Potosí, which derived its origin as a mining town. It is still a mining town, but has grown into a rail center and quite an industrial city. It also had the largest group of motels of any city we encountered on our trip.

We had selected the Cactus Motel from our AAA book, which had quoted rates from $29.00 to $35.00 for the night. They were asking $75.00, so we brought out the book and showed them that it said $29.00 to $35.00. We settled for a $35.00 room for the night. It appears they all work the same pattern —ask for $75.00, and take what the book says if you confront them. If you plan to stay in any of the hotels listed in another chapter, be sure to take the book in with you. It may save you much more than its cost.

It was an excellent motel with a very nice restaurant and even a night club. We passed on that. We had originally planned to go to Querétaro—two hours further down the road—but our mechanical troubles changed our mind.

We found a Pemex station next door, so I serviced the car and replenished our supply of ice from its mini-mart. We also stocked-up on bottled water and lunch items for the next day, plus some breakfast goodies. We planned to hit the road at 5:00 a.m.

MEXICO CITY AND CUERNAVACA

Our plans for this day were far too ambitious. We did not take into account, the two hours we lost by not getting to Querétaro the day before. We had planned to by-pass Mexico City via Puebla, then go directly to Oaxaca. At best, that would have meant a 13-hour day of driving, so we had left early to make it.

The countryside outside of San Luis Potosí was rolling farmland. The new highway seemed to by-pass most of the towns along the way. As we approached Querétaro, we were thrilled to see a lengthy Roman-type aqueduct that ran from the hill on one side of the road, to a hill on the other side. The highway ran through the arches that held up the aqueduct. I could not help but think, What a great place for someone to build a MacDonald's!

Because the highway was very good, it was just around 9:00 a.m. when we hit the morning traffic on the outskirts of Mexico City. We had been on a toll road all morning, and from the way my ears were popping and the car laboring, I could tell that we were climbing at a good rate. Of course, I knew that Mexico City was at an elevation of around 7,000 feet.

The fields between Querétaro and Mexico City were cultivated and looked quite productive. They reminded me very much like the fields of Ireland that are separated by rock fences. In this case, the fields were separated by fences made of stacked lava rock that had been taken from the fields to make room for cultivation. Volcanoes were quite visible, verifying the lava rock source. You could get a fortune for the rocks in those fences in Los Angeles.

As we neared the intersection where we were to turn off to Puebla, I could detect disappointment in my wife's face, and the fact that she had become so quiet. Mexico City was her favorite city the years she had flown on this run with American Airlines. I knew that she really wanted to see if some of her old "hang-outs" were still there. We had discussed the possibility of spending a day there, sightseeing and resting, but had ruled it out to save money. It would be a shame to be so close to her old memories, and not visit them.

When we came to the "Y" where one arrow pointed to "Puebla", and the other to "Mexico" (Mexico City is called just Mexico or Mexico, DF, and not "Mexico City"), I continued on the Mexico City route with the morning traffic. I made lots of "brownie points" with that decision. She was really back to her old excited self when we turned off onto "Avenida Reforma".

We spent an hour or so driving around her old stomping grounds where, I am sure, she used to terrorize the natives. We found her old "crew hotel", but not her favorite restaurant, the Villa Fontana.

Then I decided to put the icing on the cake, and drive down to her second favorite place, Cuernavaca, for lunch. She had always talked about the beauty of the place. From the map, it did not appear much further by taking highway 190 south to Oaxaca, than highway 131 from Puebla.

By the time we decided to go via Cuernavaca, we had no idea how to find our way through the maze of streets of downtown Mexico City to the road to Cuernavaca. We resorted to a trick we had been using when we were lost or needed directions. We spotted a little Volkswagen bug with a very nice looking young lady driving it. As we came to a traffic light, Audrey rolled down her window and caught her attention, and asked her what street to take to get to the road to Cuernavaca. She explained to Audrey, who seemed confused in trying to translate the directions to me in English while talking to her in Spanish.

The lady in the VW pulled up beside us at the next traffic light, blowing her horn and waving to Audrey. She told Audrey to follow her. Then she pulled in front of us, and meandered through town for at least five miles. Suddenly we were on a beautiful four-lane divided parkway heading out of town. She pulled over. We stopped beside her and thanked her for her trouble. She told us this was the road, and for us to watch for a turn-off several miles down the road. Then she waved good-bye, did a U-turn, and headed back to town. We were overwhelmed by her deed.

We found Cuernavaca and had lunch. The city was every bit as beautiful as Audrey had remembered. After driving around and looking at the stately mansions, we headed out of town.

After getting into and out of a traffic jam, at about 2:30 p.m. we headed for Oaxaca.

FINDING OAXACA IN THE DARK

Our next step was sheer madness. First, we knew and had agreed that we should only drive during the daylight hours. We should have accepted our time loss and headed for a hotel or motel, even if it required some back-tracking. We were too far down the road when we discovered the next sizable town had no hotel or motel. We were sort of beyond the "point of no return" at that time. The only thing we could do was to hope and pray that it would work out in our favor.

To compound our problems, we did not have enough gas to get us all of the way to Oaxaca, and we were back down to just travellers checks. It was getting dusk when we came to a little town called "Acatlán". It had no hotel or motel, but it did have a Pemex gas station.

We drove into the station and asked if the owner or boss was there. A very nice young lady came forward. Audrey explained our plight. We needed $20.00 worth of gas to get us to Oaxaca, and all we had was a $20.00 travellers check to pay for it.

She took us into the office and got on the telephone. She was obviously talking to her boss. She talked for a while, then she read every word on the travellers check, then every word on my passport. She finally got approval—but not thanks to Karl Malden. We sold this one ourselves. We put in $20.00 worth of Pemex regular (no Magna Sin), and drove off into the sunset.

As darkness fell upon us, we found ourselves on a twisting two-lane road cut into the sides of very rugged mountains, with a large number of trucks. The road had no markings, neither a center dividing line or outside markers. Fortunately, very few cars or trucks were going our way, eliminating my need to pass. We did meet a lot of them in the early evening, however. Every time we would meet one, I would pull over as close to the edge as I dared, and would dim my lights and let them pass by me.

We had been struggling along for several hours, when finally a car passed me. They apparently knew the road, as they were going much faster than I had been driving. By keeping them just ahead of me, I could get a better view of the road ahead, and was able to safely increase my speed to keep up with him. Also, it was getting so late that the trucks had stopped for the night.

It was nearly 10:00 p.m. when we came out of the mountains into a wide valley. We could see the lights of, what we assumed was Oaxaca a few miles ahead—a most welcome sight. When we arrived in town, we found the street we were on led us to the *plaza*, the park in the center of the city. Most Latin American cities are built around a *plaza*. In Mexico this central plaza is called a *zócalo*.

Once again we had selected a hotel from the AAA book. This was the Senorial Hotel, located right on the *plaza*. We did not know which side of the plaza it was on, so we found a parking place and took a stroll around the plaza to find it. Instead of streets facing the *plaza*, they just came to the four corners. A large walk-way with businesses and nearly a solid ring of sidewalk cafes faced it. Even at the late hour (to us), the cafes were filled with people dining in the moonlight with many Mariachi bands' melodies filling the night air. How we wished we had arrived earlier to have enjoyed this festive setting.

We located our hotel facing the square. When we went to check in, once again they, too, were asking $75.00 for the room. We showed them the AAA book with its $28.75 price, and miraculously the price became $28.75, and they took travellers checks. When we had parked in a secured parking lot half a block away, and entered our room, it had been seventeen hours since we left our motel in San Luis Potosí. I did not need a Mariachi band to put me to sleep.

The next morning we had a lovely breakfast downstairs in a sort of patio room. We were completely rested from our marathon drive of the day before. We checked out after cashing $100.00 in travellers checks, retrieved our van and reluctantly headed out of town. This city seemed to me, a place that I would love to see more of. I could even contemplate living here. But we had no time for sightseeing, so we headed south, out of town.

SOUTH TO THE BORDER

On the day before, after leaving Cuernavaca and entering the mountains, until it became too dark to see, the mountains and fields seemed barren and parched. The poor cattle we saw on this desolate land were looking for a blade of grass or anything to eat. Their skinny frames were witness to the fact there was not much vegetation.

Now, as we left Oaxaca, the fields were lush with green grass and plentiful crops everywhere. We were in a different world.

Shortly after leaving Oaxaca, we entered an area where there were Alp-like mountains. Rivers gushed out of canyons, with prosperous looking farms tucked along their banks wherever the canyon widened out to form a little valley.

We started noticing the sides of these mountains were terraced, somewhat similar to the mountains of the Himalayas in Western China. At first we could not figure out what sort of crops they were growing. Finally, one of the terraced fields came down to the highway, and we could see it was the type of cactus plant with large sharp spears radiating out from the its base. In a small mountain town, we saw a truck loaded with this cactus. The spears had all been cut off, leaving the root portion in a large ball. Audrey advanced the theory that the Mexicans make liquor from cactus, so we assumed this was a truckload of raw product that would eventually be used to induce many hangovers.

Later in the day, along the rivers we started seeing groves of coconut palms and bananas. We also saw farms that were surrounded by square-shaped fields of different shades of green and yellow. We met numerous trucks loaded with produce heading north. They were probably on their way to the markets of Oaxaca or Mexico City.

THE NEGATIVE SIDE OF THE TRIP

In most of Mexico and later in the Central American countries, we soon became aware of some unpleasant things which exist. One of the most noticeable was the method they use in disposing of their garbage and trash. Along the road just outside of nearly every village, town or city would be areas where the trash and garbage was brought out and apparently just thrown out of the vehicle along the side of the road. As we saw some of them burning, someone must be in charge of setting them afire. Nearly always there were dogs, children and old people combing through this refuse trying to find something useful, a treasure or a bite of uneaten food. Cholera is a big threat to this area of the world, and this would be an ideal way to spread it.

Another very unsanitary thing you will see in all of Mexico and throughout Central America, is in the toilets of the cities as well as in the rural areas. Beside the toilet will be a waste basket in which used toilet paper is thrown. They do not flush toilet paper down the sewer. If there is no basket, the paper is just thrown in the corner, behind, or beside the toilet on the floor. In public toilets along the border states such as California, Arizona, New Mexico and Texas where there is an influx of Latinos, you may have seen this practice. This could also be a way of spreading Cholera or other diseases. The United Nations needs to set up a way of re-educating these people. A few years ago we used to see sanitary re-education programs on television programs in Japan.

One of my pet peeves is not a sanitary thing—it is more a sanity item—and is something for you to watch out for in your drive through this area. That is the *"tope"*, also called *"vibradores"* or *" Reductores de velocidad"* in Central America. The *tope* is a speed bump, and they are used in the smaller towns and villages to control the speed of traffic. In Mexico, they usually have warning signs starting with, *TOPE* 300 M, *TOPE* 200 M, *TOPE* 100 M, and then right beside the speed bump is a sign with an arrow pointing down at a 45 degree angle toward the bump, with the word *TOPE*. If you do not slow down, your head will bang against the ceiling and knock your teeth out—not saying what it will do to the car. Some are so severe you must come to a complete stop before creeping over them. They are mean, so beware!

Some villages may have one at the entrance and one at the exit of the village. Larger villages may have three or four of them. What really slips up on you is the very small place with just one speed bump. You do not realize you are in a village until you hear, KER-PLOP! Then you have had it.

A typical sign warning of speed bumps or "Topes" ahead.

And of course, throughout Latin America are the ever present potholes. Even a country as advanced in education, health and industry as Costa Rica, does not take care of its potholes. They even have unmarked holes in the streets where sewers have caved in, and which are large enough to swallow your car's wheel. One of the greatest hazards is where someone has removed a manhole cover, and it stays unmarked forever. Hitting one of those could ruin your day—not to mention your wheel alignment. I would have to give Guatemala and El Salvador both credit for having the most pothole-free roads on the Pan-American Highway over which we drove.

Not until we reached Costa Rica did we discover another driving hazard. That is the police with their radar guns. The speed limits vary between 40 k.p.h. (25 m.p.h.), 60 m.p.h. (37 m.p.h.), to 80 k.p.h. (48 m.p.h.). I do remember a 100 k.p.h. (62 m.p.h.) stretch of highway somewhere along the trip. Local cars have their speed indicators calibrated in k.p.h., while most American cars have the kilometer scale inside of the m.p.h. scale. My van has small white numbers, and with my 73-year-old vision I cannot read them while driving. I have had to memorize the scale, and at age 73, that is quite an accomplishment.

When you get stopped and ticketed for speeding, the policeman comes equipped with tools to remove your license plates. The only way to get them back is to go to court and pay your fine. It has been alleged that some policemen will accept an amount less than the official fine, on the spot. You must be careful, however, because you may run into an honest cop.

As we reached the coastal plain between Tehuantepec and the Guatemalan border, we started seeing orchards of different fruits which we were not familiar to us, as well as bananas, citrus and coconut palms. Later we found that the unfamiliar fruit trees were to become our favorite tropical fruit —the mango.

The roads were very straight, and we were able to hit speeds of 65 to 75 m.p.h., but we had to be constantly alert for the speed bumps and potholes.

We arrived at the border city of Tapachula, Mexico in the late afternoon, and found a very clean, fairly new motel at the exit end of town, at a very reasonable rate. We preferred motels because we could usually park right in front of our room and unload what we needed for the night, including our ice chest which we had to clean and replenish with ice, sandwich makings, yogurt, fruit and drinks.

Talking about drinks, there are grocery stores in every town or city, which have bottled water and packaged cheese and sandwich meats. As I successfully did in China for years—eat only fruit that you can peel, and beware of ice cubes. We had no trouble with "tourista" sometimes also called "Montezuma's Revenge". In medical terms this illness is known as dysentery. Just drink bottled water and sodas and you should have no problem. However watch out for ice cubes made with unpurified water. Speaking of ice, here is a handy advice for your ice chest. Get one of those rectangular plastic dishes with a tight fitting lid. Put your ice cubes in it. That keeps the melted ice from spoiling your food.

That night, the Saturday night before the Super Bowl, we had dinner in a restaurant down the street. They had a big screen TV and big signs inviting everyone to come there for the Super Bowl Party. It might have been tempting to us if the 49ers, the Rams or the Raiders were playing. But without them, why waste our time?

After dinner, it was such a nice warm evening that we stopped off at an ice cream parlor down the street from the motel for a couple of *"conos"* or cones. While seated at an outside table, we started talking to a very nice English-speaking Mexican who was there with his lovely wife and adorable baby. We mentioned that we planned to take the more direct coastal route through Guatemala to San Salvador the next day. He suggested that the road through Guatemala City, which was a little longer route but much better and faster than the coastal route. We decided to take his advise and thanked him very much for his help. Later, we even thanked him more, and thanked god for sending him our way. We were not aware of that, however, until two days later in Honduras.

DRIVING ACROSS GUATEMALA

After a good night's sleep, in spite of our having to break up a pre-Super Bowl party outside of our door at 2:00 a.m., we were up at 5:00 a.m. and on our way. We really hoped to drive through Guatemala and El Salvador to Choluteca, Honduras that day. That would mean six border crossings in one day, plus nine hours of driving. I figured that we would surely have to cut it shorter than that.

We crossed the Mexican border at 5:30 a.m. with no problem. We had been told that the border was open all night. Not so.

Incidentally, carry a large manila envelope with you. As you cross a border into a country, put all of the papers they give you into that envelope. As you come to the check point where you leave that country, the guards will want some or all of the papers you have. If there are any left over, put them in another safe place and hold on to them until you reach your destination. Then use the manila envelope for that country, and so on. After you get to your destination, you can "round file" everything except the entry papers of your destination country. Hang onto them. You will probably need them later.

Even though we had been told the border would be open 24 hours a day, we found that it did not open until 7:00 a.m.. About 6:00 a.m. two cars from California pulled in behind us at the inspection station. Both drivers spoke fluent Spanish and had driven the route before. One of them told me to make a list of the contents of each box and suitcase, which I did while waiting.

The Guatemalan border guards showed up at 7:00 a.m., and the two Spanish-speaking Californians used their ability to communicate to push by me. They were out of there by 7:30 a.m.. Meanwhile a nice lady guard started processing us. We had one big problem. We did not have either U.S. or Guatemalan currency—and had used all of our Mexican *pesos* as we figured we would not need them. We only had travellers checks. Remember, you will need up to $50.00 for each border crossing, either in U.S. or local currency.

While the lady guard was typing up our papers, Audrey had been trying out her Spanish on one of the guards—a senior citizen-type. He was curious as to why I kept talking into my little tape recorder. She told him that I was planning to write a book about our trip, and was dictating my notes into the recorder. About that time I needed some cash to pay for our entry. No one would take travellers checks. We were about to have to go back to the motel in Mexico for more money, when Audrey told the guard of our predicament. He said he would cash a $50.00 travellers check for us, so Audrey called him an "Earth Angel". When he gave me the money, he told me to be sure to mention his name in my book.

So for all of you checking through the Guatemalan border at Tapachula, be sure to pick yourself up some "Brownie Points" by asking for Joe Garcia and tell him you read about what an "Earth Angel" he is in my book. Incidentally, he tried to talk us into staying over and come to his house for dinner.

Meanwhile I paid my fees, the lady checked our car, looked at the packing list I had made, and put a nice green sticker on our windshield, and we were off into Guatemala. We came to a customs check point just a ways down the road where we discovered the two California cars pulled off, with all of their bags on the ground beside their cars, being inspected. The guards just looked at our papers and waved us through. The Californians watched us drive off in envy. Their pushing through tactics had backfired on them. Incidentally, we would meet one of them again at the border into Nicaragua.

MORE ABOUT BORDER CROSSINGS

At this point we would like to interrupt our trip to add a little more about the border crossings we mention in Chapter 1.

As you approach a border, you will come to the money changers. As you leave one country to enter the next one, you may have currency left over from the country you are leaving, and will need local currency (about $50.00 worth) to get through the new country border. Unless you are returning soon, change the unneeded local money and buy additional currency with some of the U.S. dollars you have stashed away for this purpose. There are no banks at the crossings so that is your best bet, unless you have previously purchased your $50.00 minimum for each country in advance. Karl Mallden has no arrangements for you to cash travellers checks at the borders.

A tollbooth on the Pan-American Highway.

As soon as you get through the money changers, you will be hit by a bunch of youths who will run alongside of your car talking in Spanish. Some enterprising ones speak English. They are trying to get you to hire them to guide you through the border check points. There are usually about six stations at each border check, and not necessarily in any logical order. I really think they have so many check points so you can "pay off" each one, which would help their economy. At some borders they have posted the fee of only $1.50, but don't you believe it. The kids are worth the little tip that you give them for guiding you through.

Your guide will ask you for certain papers, which he takes to the various stations, and he will tell you how much you are to pay the guard. Grin, bear it and pay! When you are through all of your check points, tip your guide. I suppose a couple of dollars is all right. I seem to always overtip and give my guide up to $5.00 in local currency if he has done a good fast job. Let him know in advance that you will pay more for a fast check-out job. As we have alluded to several times, these helpers are indispensable at border crossings. They will save you a lot of time and grief.

BACK TO GUATEMALA

Our first impression of Guatemala was that the vegetation near the border crossing was more tropical than in Mexico. Quite a big change, after travelling only a short distance. This jungle was soon replaced by farms.

The greatest change was the difference in the people. One would think that changes in people and culture would be gradual as you travel from one country to the next. But here it was like walking through a door into another world. First, there were more people walking along the roads or riding the more frequent numbers of buses than in Mexico. The early morning roads were crowded.

There were women in brilliantly colored clothing, carrying bundles, jugs, boxes and bundles of wood on their heads. They had a sort of towel curled on top of their head, making a platform for the load they were carrying. They walked down the road very erect, not using their hands to hold the load in place.

Then the numbers of people crowding into and on to each bus had to be seen to be believed. On a normal forty-passenger bus there would be at least one hundred passengers jammed inside. Others would be hanging on the outside of the buses, hanging onto the window frames and the doors with their feet flying into the air. Others would be on top of the bus. I judged that there had to be in excess of one hunderd twenty-five people in, on and around each forty-passenger bus. I could not figure how they were possibly able to collect the fares.

In Mexico the roads are very well marked, both by the road numbers and the next major city, with the distance in kilometers. The quick conversion factor from kilometers to miles is to multiply the kilometers by .62. I would round it off to .6, mentally, and come up with a good mileage estimate and add or subtract a bit. From the time you leave Mexico until you get to Costa Rica where again the roads are again well marked, you are in a "by guess and by god" situation.

When you come to an intersection where you should go one way or another, you choose the one you think it might be, then right away ask someone the right way. Use the name of major cities or countries when you ask them. Then, when you are in the direction they told you, ask another person down the road a ways. You will be amazed at how some of them will go into a five-minute dissertation, pointing in one direction and seem so sincere, yet be wrong. They seem to get confused over little things. For instance, let's assume you are trying to get to Guatemala City, and you ask a local, "Is this the way to Guatemala City?" Don 't use so many words. Just point and say, "Guatemala?" in the form of a question. If you say "Guatemala City?", he is already confused. He does not know what the word "city" means. They just call it Guatemala. When you throw in too many other words, he will be trying to figure out what they all mean, and again he is confused. So, just be as brief as possible.

In one case shortly after we entered Guatemala, the road we were on, dead-ended on what seemed to be a main road. Both directions seemed to indicate about equal tire wear, so we had to guess . I turned right. A quarter mile down the road, I asked someone, and he pointed in the opposite direction. So, I made a "U-turn" and went the other way. Then I asked another man down the road, and he pointed in the direction I was going and said, "*directo, directo*", which means "straight ahead" in Spanish. Later, in studying the map, the other direction was the coastal road which we had originally picked, until the man at the ice cream parlor in Tapachula changed our mind.

The road to Guatemala City took us through beautiful farmland with many dairies which had healthy looking herds. The whole area appeared to be very prosperous.

As we drove into the outskirts of Guatemala City, our map indicated that we did not need to go into the center of the city. Of course, we were using the National Geographic map, and not a regular road map. We were on a four-lane divided highway with a chain-link fence down the center median. Suddenly we saw a beautiful new Shell station on the other side of the fence. It had, of all things, a Circle-K mini-mart. We saw this as a possible stop. It gave us an opportunity to service the car, refill our ice chest with ice and goodies, use possibly new, clean rest-rooms and even cash a travellers check, all in one stop.

We managed to turn around at an intersection, and made our way back to the station. They accepted a travellers check (thank you, Karl). So, while I serviced the car, Audrey used their "facilities", then went in to shop. When I was through with the car and my "pit stop", I went into the store. Audrey was all excited. She was talking to a nice lady who was trying to draw her a map, showing her how to get on the road to San Salvador without going down town. Her problem was that she was not a cartographer, and was not doing too well with the map.

Suddenly, she threw up her hands in disgust and told us to follow her, and she would show us the right way. Shades of Mexico City and the lady in the VW bug.

She went out and jumped into her new Nissan Stanza. We forgot our shopping, and ran after her to follow her in our van. She did a U-turn around the other end of the chain-link fence, then went off into an industrial area, zigging here, zagging there for about five miles. Suddenly we popped out onto another four-lane divided highway and she told us to go, "*directo, directo*", so we thanked her and continued straight ahead.

Again as in Mexico City, we were amazed that she would go out of her way for strangers—on a Sunday morning. It made me wonder how many Americans would have done such a generous thing?

We debated about missing our opportunity to shop in the Shell mini-mart. No more than a mile down the road was a new Texaco station, with yet another Circle-K. We pulled in and completed our shopping and refilling of our ice chest. Wow! This was almost as though we had not left the states. I paid with the change from cashing the travellers check at the Shell station.

The highway was much better than anything we had seen in Mexico, allowing us to drive 65 to 75 m.p.h. After leaving Guatemala City, we came into an area with vast fields of sugar cane. We also ran into a lot of trucks loaded with cut sugar cane, heading for the sugar mill somewhere up ahead. The road was straight and wide, so we had no trouble passing them.

ACTUAL TRIP ALONG THE PAN-AMERICAN HIGHWAY

We soon came to a gigantic sugar mill. Trucks loaded with cane were lined up for at least a mile, waiting their turn on the scales and to unload their cargo. Everything about the area of Guatemala we had gone through indicated wealth and affluence, which really surprised me. On the edge of my National Geographic map, there were boxes that gave their G.N.P. and per-capita income for each Central American country. Again, we were surprised to see that Guatemala was second to Panama in income, and Costa Rica, which we had assumed would be number one, came in third.

INTO PEACEFUL EL SALVADOR

We went through Guatemala with no problems. We had changed our Guatemalan currency to Salvadorian as we left Guatemala. By the time we got through the El Salvador border check, I did not have enough local money left to give the guide a decent tip.

At the El Salvadorian check point, the guard wanted us to unload our van for customs inspection. Audrey went right to work and had three boxes off-loaded, when I got the guard and showed him my list that I had made. After looking in the three boxes and glancing under the bed, he said, "OK", and waved us through. So, be sure to make up your inventory list, and have it translated into Spanish, if possible.

The road from the border to San Salvador was another high-speed divided four-lane toll road. As we approached our first toll plaza, I realized that we had used all of our Salvadorian currency at the border. Then we got to the toll booth, I showed the toll-taker a $50.00 travellers check and told him that was all I had. He shook his head, waived us through, and said, "See you later, Joe". The next tolltaker also just waved us through.

We called it a day when we arrived in San Salvador, which was recently so hostile to the United States. It was one country that I was concerned about entering. Yet we left with the feeling of being not only accepted, but quite welcome.

We had not really planned on staying here, but we were nearly half a day behind our schedule, so we played the cards as they were dealt. As we entered the city, there was another one of those super Texaco stations with its most welcome Circle-K mini-market. We inquired if there was a motel nearby, and were directed to a hotel just a block away. We parked in front and registered, and were told to drive along the side of the hotel and park in the basement garage.

We were able to load our luggage directly into the elevator which would take us right to our floor and room. For all of this, our cost was $39.00. They cashed $100.00 extra in travellers checks. We thought this amount would last us until we reached Costa Rica.

There was a picturesque dining room where we had a delightful dinner. After a good night's sleep, we left at 5:00 a.m., and drove to the Texaco station. While I serviced the car, Audrey shopped for our breakfast and more goodies for the ice chest. Then I just followed the Budget Rent-a-Car map the hotel clerk had given to me, and we headed out of San Salvador and south once again. As we were departing the city we had quite a surprise. We had expected to see a war-ravaged city such as some of the cities we had seen in Germany after World War II.

Not so! The whole downtown area was built up with brand new high-rise buildings. Even the older part of town along "mansion row" as we left the city, was unharmed and in beautiful shape. Was this, perhaps, where the millions that the United States sent to help fight the war, went?

HONDURAS AND THE NICARAGUAN BORDER

Our amended goal for this day was to drive across the other half of El Salvador, through the short neck of Honduras, and into Managua, which was about half way across Nicaragua.

We made it out of El Salvador with no difficulty, but when we got to the Honduras border check, things changed. The problem was with a very nasty soldier who insisted that we take everything out of the van for him to check. I showed him the list, but to no avail. He insisted. He had us back up to a concrete loading dock. There was a crew of about twenty-five eager helpers who were going to pick up some easy money from the *"gringo"*. The other part of the problem was that this *"gringo"* had gone through a similar mob-type action in China before this soldier was born.

He let me know that he wanted me to pick out a crew to unload the van. We were in the boiling hot sun. I balked. I made him understand that I wanted him to get everyone back to the far edge of the concrete platform. I stood and waited for him to do as I promised. He finally relented and got them back, after I suggested that he had no control over the situation. I had such an incident in China, where we got everything exposed, and then the Chinese mob grabbed everything and ran off in different directions. I was not about to have a repeat of that type of action.

I unloaded the mattress and the bedding against a pole on the platform. Audrey was unloading through the side door of the van and I was taking the mattress out of the back. When we had all of the boxes and suitcases unloaded, he insisted that I take out the bed springs. With a bit of pantomiming, I got through to him that first, the bed springs were solidly fixed to the van (if I had moved the front seats forward a bit, it would have come right out), and second that he could see there was nothing under the springs. After I had backed him down twice, his potential loading crew started razzing him. I think he was ready to get rid of us.

He opened and looked into three boxes, then motioned for us to load up and get out. We did not hesitate, but started loading the van immediately. He was standing, watching us with a sneer on his face. We got into the van and made some fast tracks out of there.

One thing that had been puzzling us since we were in Southern Mexico, was that quite often, and with apparently nothing to do with the town dumps, we would see another type of roadside litter. This appeared to be blue plastic sheets strewn along the road. We could not figure it out, until suddenly we came upon a banana grove beside the road. Over each bunch of bananas on the trees was one of these blue plastic bags, tied to secure the bunch at the top.

We asked about this during our lunch stop, and found out that the bags were put over the bunches of bananas to protect them from insects, birds and other banana lovers. Then they pick the bananas, the bags are stripped off and just dumped along the road. I guess the farmers do not want to litter their fields with them. (I see in the papers where Costa Rica has taken action to stop this practice in its country).

We came to the town of Choluteca, Honduras right at noon. It was only twenty-five miles from the Nicaraguan border, and just about two hours from there to Managua. There was no possible way to make it to Costa Rica this day, so we decided to treat ourselves.

We stopped at a very nice hotel and restaurant called the Hotel La Fonte, right on the Pan-American Highway in the center of town. We decided to have our first "sit-down" lunch since we left Laredo, Texas. We had lunch, and changed another $50.00 travellers check. After lunch we gassed up and headed for the border.

THE NICARAGUAN BORDER CRISIS

We checked out through the Honduran border wihtout any problems. It was just 1:15 p.m. when we arrived at the Nicaraguan border check point. When we went in to clear customs, we were told that they closed at 1:00 p.m. and we should return the next morning at 7:00 a.m.

We were just getting ready to go back to Choluteca and have a relaxing afternoon by the pool, when the same Americans (Spanish speaking) from California who had pushed in front of us at the Guatemalan border, drove up. We told them what we had been told. One of them said it would be easy to get across the border and he would bribe us through. Even though he spoke good Spanish, he got nowhere. After being turned down at every department at the checkpoint, he came back to discuss the situation with us. There were three in his party—himself, his wife and his wife's sister. They were driving the sister to Panama in her Toyota long bed pickup with a shell covering the back. They had driven from El Monte, California.

They asked us what we were going to do. We told them we were going back to Choluteca and stay at the motel where we had lunch. They said they would follow us back. I was sure that we got registered and did not let him slip in front of us again. We got to our room with time for a good rest before dinner.

We all joined for dinner, where they told us a story that made us thank the nice Mexican man at the ice cream parlor in Tapachula, even more than before.

We had originally intended to take the coast road through Guatemala, but this wonderful man talked us out of it. This group who had cut in front of us at the border, and who we last saw at the customs having their load checked as we were waved through, took the coastal road.

At the point where we had turned off to Guatemala City, they took the coastal road for a few miles when they came to a village. The locals were all lined up along the main street waving at them. They thought it was a nice welcoming gesture, so they waved back and drove on through.

Just a couple of miles down the road, they were stopped by a tank in the middle of the road. They heard gunfire and discovered the Guatemalan army was on one side of the road, and an army of guerrillas was on the other, and they were caught in the middle. They were using everything—rifles, machine guns, bazookas and artillery.

These poor people were scared out of their wits. They were hunched down in their car, and had just about given up hope of getting out alive. A soldier was shot right in front of their car as he ran across the road. They could see where the bullet entered his back, and the blood spurting out of his chest where the bullet left his body. He took a few steps, then fell down forward, presumably dead. Suddenly the tank pulled off the road into a field so they started their car and raced safely away from their near demise.

If not for the good advice from the man in Mexico, we would have been there, too.

The next morning at 6:00 a.m., we formed a two car caravan and headed for the border. We were cleared with no problem, but the customs officials made our friends completely unload their covered pickup and the luggage rack on the top. We wanted to get through the Nicaraguan exit border before 10:00 p.m.—just in case they also closed early.

We bid our new friends farewell and raced across Nicaragua nonstop. We crossed over into Costa Rica well before 1:00 p.m..

Please make a note, if your plans include driving through Nicaragua, get through the border crossings before 1:00 p.m.—just in case.

HOME AT LAST - IN COSTA RICA

The treatment we received as we crossed the Costa Rican border was the best one of the trip. We did not run into the deal of having several check points. It was so easy compared to the other crossings.

We drove a few miles into Costa Rica to the first sizable town, Liberia,where we stopped for fuel. We also found an ice cream parlor from which we called our new landlord. We told him to plug in the refrigerator and that we would be "home" by 7:00 p.m..

We pulled into the driveway at 7:15 p.m.. We checked our speed-ometer, and we had traveled exactly 4,200 miles from our driveway in El Toro, California to our new home in San José de la Montaña in just 10 days of driving.

So, if a seventy-three-year-old senior citizen ,with a leaking replacement heart valve and a pacemaker, can drive the Pan-American Highway with very few problems, What do you think of your chances?

CHAPTER V

OTHER PEOPLE'S TRIPS ON THE PAN-AMERICAN HIGHWAY

After publishing the first edition of this book in 1992, we received numerous suggestions that we include accounts of other people's trips along the Pan-American Highway in future editions of this guidebook. While I was contemplating where I could get more current information, I received a letter from Laurie Gonzáles, manager of the Belén Trailer Park located off Highway 1, between the International Airport and the city of San José, Costa Rica. Since that is only about five miles from my home, I decided to drive over and check it out.

When I arrived at the trailer park, I found it was bustling with activity. There was a caravan of seventeen recreation vehicles that were making a tour of Central America, and were on their way to Panama the following day. The manager, a very nice American lady, who had lived in Costa Rica for about 10 years, told me the RV owners would be stopping over for a few days on their way back up north. So, I decided to interview another couple who had been there for a while longer. You can read about their journey on the next page.

If you have recently driven through Mexico or Central America by car, RV or camper, why don't you share your story with others who would like to hear the details of your trip. Send us your story, and please include information about the RV parks, campgrounds or hotels where you stayed. Please include as much information as possible about facilities, costs, etc.. Include any printed material you may have picked-up such as brochures. We will put your information into a story format, and return it for your approval. Acknowledgement will be given for your efforts.

LAS VEGAS TO COSTA RICA

This story was told to me by Lou and Celine Gregoire, formerly of Las Vegas, Nevada. It took place in the spring of 1992.

They drove from Las Vegas to the border crossing at Nogales, Arizona. There they met with two groups of Missionaries who were trying to get cleared into Mexico on their way to Guatemala. It took them two days to get their visas, which verifies the statement in Chapter I — that it is best to get your visas from an embassy before you start out on your trip. The Gregoires decided to join up with them, as it appeared it would be more fun, and with the "safety in numbers" idea in mind, they would all feel safer. None of them had made the trip before.

They drove down the coastal highway. They found that it was very hot—usually in the mid-90s to as much as 110 degrees. The roads were quite rough and filled with many potholes. They do not recommend that route for anyone, unless they like the heat. From, the map, one would think it would have nice ocean breezes, as it follows the coast. Not so!

One group of missionaries was driving a Suburban and were pulling a trailer. About halfway throuth Mexico, their trailer hitch broke. They happened to be near a village that had a welding shop, so they were able to get it fixed and start on their way again.

Late in the afternoon, when they found a spot they liked, they would stop for the night. As their vehicles were self-contained, it was only necessary for them to stop for servicing their toilets every other day or so. In addition to the Suburban, the missionaries also had a converted bus with all facilities, including water tanks, holding tanks and kitchen. In most cases, their only requirement for a stop was to find a level spot to park.

They had no real problems in Mexico, but when they arrived at the

Guatemalan border crossing, they ran into trouble. It was a Saturday morning, and they had no visas. The office where they were to pick up their visas was closed until Monday, so they were in a jam. They had the choice of returning to Tapachula, Mexico, or stay on the International bridge until they could get cleared. Not wanting to backtrack, they opted to stay where they were.

Prospects looked very bleak. They were uncomfortable in the 110 degree heat, nearly out of food, and all felt dirty and in need of a bath. One of the group did some scouting and made contact with an off-duty immigration officer who came down on his own time to clear them. I wondered if it was good old "Joe Garcia"—Audrey's "Earth Angel" who was so kind to us on our crossing of this border.

No sooner had the visa problem been solved than they faced another challenge. The Guatemalan customs officer was very clear that he did not like Christians, and missionaries in particular. He put the Suburban and the bus into quarantine, and was not going to allow them into the country. Another "Earth Angel" came to their rescue. The head boss and the customs officer got into a heated argument, with the boss ruling in favor of the missionaries. He not only gave them clearance here, but also gave them clearance papers through all of the military check points they would come to in Guatemala to their destination of Zacapa.

The Gregoires left the missionaries at that point, and continued by themselves. They took the coastal route to El Salvador, where they stayed in San Salvador for the night.

In San Salvador, they had a flat tire on their trailer. Lou got out to fix it, and was suddenly surrounded by several taxi drivers, who brought out their equipment and proceeded to change the tire for him. When he offered to pay them for their trouble, they refused to accept payments stating they were glad to help the *"Americanos"* who had helped them during their civil war.

They had no problems crossing into Honduras or Nicaragua. Their next challenge occured when they crossed into Costa Rica. In the other countries the customs officers would glance into their trailer, look into a box or two in their pickup, and wave them on through. The Costa Rican authorities were a little more thorough.

They checked their pickup shell very carefully, and discovered four unmounted tires. They confiscated them on the grounds that they were a hazardous breeding ground for mosquitoes. At the U.S. price of $60.00 each, and the Costa Rican price three or four times that amount, Lou stood to lose a lot of money. They had three days to get the tires mounted or have them confiscated. There was a station nearby that would sell them the wheels, and mount them. The other choice was to just go off and leave them for the officials to dispose of. This procedure smelled of "scam" to me, but it is Costa Rican law, and they were now in Costa Rica. I wondered if they had packed them into those black garbage bags, if they would have gotten away with it. One fellow circumvented their code by having blown-up tubes in each of the tires.

From the border check they drove on to Liberia, the first sizable town in Costa Rica. They stayed at the Hotel Guanacaste Travel Lodge which had facilities for recreation vehicles, where they stayed for the night. The next day they drove into the Belén RV Park, located in San Antonio de Belén. They had been there some time when I met them.

They have obtained their *Pensionado* status, and are in the process of buying a *finca* (ranch or farm) on the Caribbean coast.

Thank you Lou and Celine for the great story, and let's hope that someone reading this book will profit from your experiences, as well as your good fortune.

CALIFORNIA TO PANAMA VIA NOGALES

Tony and Jim, two Californians we interviewed, made a trip from Los Angeles to Panama City by car. They left Los Angeles early one morning and drove to Tuscon, Arizona in their 1968 VW van. The next morning the entered Mexico at Nogales. Customs was a breeze and the drove all the way to the port of Guaymas. From there they went to Mazatlán to relax and soak up some rays for a couple of days. They camped at a nice trailer park right on the beach.

While relaxing in Mazatlán, they decided they were going to try to drive to Panama as quickly as possible but vowed they wouldn't drive at night. After working on their tans for two days in Mazatlán, they left for Guadaljara and arrived later the same day. The next day the made it all the way to Cuernavaca on the outskirts of Mexico City. The follwing morning, they got up at 4 am and drove to the city of Oaxaca. Their generator had to be replaced so they lost about three hours but started out for Tapacula at 11:30 am. They found a motel as soon as it got dark and spent the night. At dawn the next day they reached the border with Guatemala. After spending the night in Tapachula they crossed over to Guatemala as soon as the border opened and made it all the way to San Salvador in one day. The next day they again left bright and early and arrived in Nicaragua. The following day they made it to San José, Costa Rica and one day later to Panama City. The last leg proved to be a grueling 16 hour drive.

Aside form the usual delays at the borders they didn't encounter any real problems. They regretted not having stopped to enjoy many of the sights along they way, so on the return trip they took their time.

A TRIP DOWN MEXICO'S EAST COAST

A friend of ours from Nevada has driven back and forth between Costa Rica and his home in Nevada about six times. A couple of times with friends and the other times alone. No he's not crazy. He just likes to spend about six months a year in Costa Rica and wants to have a vehicle while he is there. He swares by the Brownsville route down the East Coast of Mexico, cuting across the isthmus and them proceding into Central America. By taking this route he avoids 1,500 miles of Mexican highway. He makes the 4,500 mile trip fom Nevada in 11 days driving from sunrise to almost sundown. He always insures his vehicle through Mexico and Central America stopping at a Sanborn's office in Texas.

Since he has made the trip so many times he doesn't stop and see the sights. He claims the most important thing is to get a good nights sleep, get up early and leave from all border crossings as early as possible. He really recommends using the runners at the borders to speed things up. He says if it wasn't for the delays at the borders he could easily cut a couple of days off the trip. His other complaint is that there are some really bad strethces of road along the way. There is one stretch in Nicaraga where he had to drive about 20 m.p.h. for several hours because of the poor condition of the road.

He highly recommends the costal route through Guatemala and Salvador to bypass the big cities and save time. He put a motion alarm on his car, pays a watchman when he stops for the night and parks near his room. That way he says he doesn't have to unload his whole car every night. He gives the watchman a dollar or two and doesn't have to worry. Nothing has every been robbed from his car at night while travelling through Mexico and Central America.

TO COSTA RICA BUY BUS

Ralph Henneman form the U. S. recounted his long journey and experiences while driving the Pan-American Highway to Río Frío, Costa Rica in late 1995.

He left for Costa Rica from the U.S. driving a 1971 International bus loaded with personal belongings, household goods and tools for his construction work. His 1976 Chevy van was driven at the same time by a friend who had already made the trip quite a few times. They stayed together all the way and only got separated in heavy rush hour traffic once while in Austin, Texas.

In Mexico he hit a bus in the rear due to the other buse's break failure. Luckily there was only little bumper damage and he gave his Mexican Insurance to the bus driver. However, in Guatemala the bus developed a radiator leak as a result of the accident in Mexico. They found a garage soon after the motor started heating up. The mechanic took the radiator out and repaired the leak. Then put it in and only charged $20. His friend found a motel for $10 a night with a swimming pool and first-class room, so they stayed the night in Guatemala City.

The trip through Honduras was very slow and mountainous. They had a soldier armed with a semi-automatic in the bus all the way through the country. The same thing happened in Nicaragua. The purpose of this escort was so they couldn't sell anything on the bus.

The whole trip took 22 days with 4 days in McAllen, Texas due to problems with customs at the Mexican border. One whole day was spent unloading almost everything on the bus and then reloading because they were moving to Costa Rica. Since the the bus was full of household goods, tools and clothing they had to pay $400 at Mexican customs.

A lot can be learned form Ralph' s many delays. You should avoid taking a lot of personal belongings while travelling through Mexico and Central America. If you are planning to move to one of these countries it is best ship your belongings by plane or in a container by boat. You will experience many hassles, untimely delays and pay a lot of taxes if you don't. They should have also taken the costal route through Guatemala and El Salvador and not traveled through the upper part of Honduras.

COSTA RICA IN FOUR DAYS BY BUS

This story is slightly crazy but true. Richard Krug, a friend of ours, bought an old Greyhound bus in California to take to Costa Rica so he could start a charter tour company. He customized and completely refurbished it: repainting it, installing spacious airplane seats, putting in a bar with a small refrigerator and a good stereo system. Together with three helpers, he drove the bus to Costa Rica in just a little over four days including border stops.

How did they accomplish this feat? What they did was drive in four hour shifts so as to not get too tired. Two people slept while one drove and the other person kept him company so he wouldn't fall asleep at the wheel. They only stopped for, gas, food and other necessities along the way.

Pesonally we think they were foolish to drive at night because of livestock that may stray onto the road. We heard of a couple of case where people collided with cows and completely destroyed their cars. People have even been killed as a result of accidents with livestock.

Poor lighting and many desolate stretches of highway also pose a danger. You also increase your chances of getting robbed if you drive when it is dark. We have heard several horror stories with sad endings about people who were assaulted while driving through Mexico and Central America at night.

FROM TEXAS TO COSTA RICA WITH A 4,000 POUND TRAILER

We have had letters from some readers who are interested in pulling a trailer down to Central America. This little story may help them. We have abbreviated it, just recounting the parts that may interest you.

This story was told to me by a man who is now my neighbor and good friend, Arzinia Richardson, and took place in 1994.

Arzinia, his lovely wife and two teen-aged daughters decided to move from Oregon to Costa Rica. They decided to pull a 4,000 pound trailer with their "goodies" that they wanted in their new home. They had a Suburban and a modified trailer. Arzinia is a sort of "Jack-of-all trades" type of fellow. He is highly educated and has taught his favorite subject—Egyptology. His wife is a registered nurse. They are not rich, but had saved their dimes and nickles for this sojourn to paradise. As they had lived and travelled to many other countries, they could "roll with the punches" with anything they might encounter on their trip.

Arzinia has a lot of mechanical aptitude, so he modified his Suburban for the trip. He "beefed up" the car and the trailer to withstand the rugged trip he knew was ahead of him. Even so, on the segment of his trip from Oregon to Brownsville his trailer hitch broke, so he repaired it at a welding shop en route.

Their trip through Mexico was uneventful. He said he felt like an attraction, however, as the locals were not used to seeing an Afro-American travelling with such good equipment as they had. At no time did they have to unload the trailer for inspection. At one point, the inspection problem was solved by the customs officials in an interesting way. They put a soldier in the car with them, and they had to take care of feeding and providing lodging for him until the check point where they left the country. Customs wanted to be sure that nothing was sold or left behind in their country. Every border check was trouble-free, and they had only one mechanical problem that Arzinia was able to take care of himself.

His advice is for you to be sure your trailer hitch is strong and that you take care in balancing your load so it will trail properly. Also, be sure that your vehicle has plenty of horsepower. It is best that the vehicle have a stick shift, and be a four-wheel drive, if possible. You can get by with a two-wheel drive, but you will have to take it easy.

There is one more important thing to remember. Be sure to have a set of tools—a ratchet set in both metric and inches, and the usual - hammer, screw drivers, etc., just like we mention in the first chapter.

One other precaution that Arzinia took, was to equip his car with "bullet proof tires". I do not think you need to go that far, but be sure you do have heavy-duty tires. It is best if the tires on your car and trailer are interchangeable to cover any problem you might have with spares.

Thank you, Arzinia, for being such a good neighbor and for sharing your experiences with us. We hope you have learned something about travelling on the Pan-American Highway from these accounts.

CHAPTER VI

HOTEL RATES AND FACILITIES

This chapter covers accommodations in Mexico and Central America found along the Pan-American Highway and other routes. When possible listings include street addresses, telephone and fax numbers, rates and facilities. Some hotels have seasonal rates, and others do not. If seasonal, both high and low rates are listed with inclusive dates for each season. We have done our best to include affordable accomodations for budget-conscious travelers. However, it is impossible to list all of the hoteles along each one of the routes in scope of this book. The guides we list in the back of this book have more complete sections on lodging.

When checking into a hotel, it is advisable to take a guidebook with you. At times, some hotels will try to get a higher rate, but should honor the book rate. If the desk clerk gives you a hard time, show him where the book quotes a different price than they have quoted you. If you run into any discrepancies, please make a note of them and contact us, at our address listed in this book.

If you stay at either a hotel or motel which doesn't appear in this guide, please obtain their brochure and send it to the publisher at the address in the front of this book. Thank you for your cooperation, and have an enjoyable and safe trip.

MEXICO HOTEL AND MOTEL RATES

**(RV)ACAPULCO, GRO, MEXICO   Economy
ACAPULCO TRAILER PARK
P.O. Box 1, Acapulco, Guerrero 14 km northwest off Mexican Highway 200
    Tel: 74/60-0010
RATES: $12.00 per night
FACILITIES: Full hookups, 80 sights,laundry, flush toilets, most sites face ocean.

ACAPULCO, GRO., 39670, MEXICO   Economy
BALI-HAI HOTEL
Ave. Costera M. Aleman 186
    Tel. (74) 85 6622 FAX: (74) 85 7972
RATES: Seasonal: Dec.16 - Apr. 20
    Single: $66.00   Double: $66.00   Extra: $20.00
RATES: Seasonal: Apr. 21 - Dec. 15
    Single: $53.00   Double: $53.00   Extra: $16.00
FACILITIES: Two pools, wading pool, restaurant nearby, refrigerators, shower & tub baths, no pets, no T.V.'s.

ACAPULCO, GRO., 39840, MEXICO   First Class
DAYS HOTEL ROMANO
Ave. Costera M. Aleman 2310
    Tel. (74) 84 5332 FAX: (74) 84 5822
RATES: Seasonal: Dec. 16 - Apr. 15
    Single: $95.00   Double: $95.00   Extra: $10.00
RATES: Seasonal: Apr. 16 - Dec. 15
    Single: $60.00   Double: $60.00   Extra: $8.00
FACILITIES: Beach, pool, dining & entertainment, free movies in room, cable T.V.

ACAPULCO, GRO., 39300, MEXICO   First Class
EL TROPICANO HOTEL
Ave. Costera M. Aleman 20
Tel: (74) 84 1100 FAX: (74) 84 1308
RATES: Seasonal: Dec. 16 - Apr. 30
Single: $58.00 Double: $58.00 Extra: $12.00
RATES: Seasonal: May 01 - Dec. 15
Single: $38.00 Double: $38.00 Extra: $10.00
FACILITIES: No pets, 2 pools, restaurant, entertainment.

One of the better hotels along the Pan-American Highway.

ACAPULCO, GRO., 39360, MEXICO   First Class
HOTEL ACAPULCO IMPERIAL
Ave. Costera M. Aleman 251 P.O. Box 688
    Tel: (74) 85 1759   FAX: (74) 83 0575
RATES: Seasonal: Dec. 20 - Apr. 30
    Single: $55.00 Double: $70.00 Extra: $12.00
RATES: Seasonal: May 1 - Dec. 19
    Single: $40.00 Double: $40.00 Extra: $12.00
FACILITIES: No pets, 2 bedroom units, wading pool, dining room, coin laundry, rental boats & water skiing, bars, shower baths, no T.V.

ACAPULCO, GRO., 39690, MEXICO   First Class
HOTEL PANORAMIC
Ave. Condesa 1
    Tel: (74) 84 0724 FAX: (74) 84 8639
RATES: Seasonal: Dec. 15 - Apr. 15
    Single: $65.00   Double: $65.00 Extra: $20.00
RATES: Seasonal: Apr. 16 - Dec. 14
    Single: $40.00   Double: $40.00 Extra: $20.00
FACILITIES: No pets, 2 pools, wading pool, 3 tennis courts (fee), restaurant, coffee shop, cocktails, cable T.V.

ACAPULCO, GRO., 39580, MEXICO   First Class
HOTEL RITZ ACAPULCO

Ave. Costera M. Aleman 159
  Tel: (74) 84 7336 FAX: (74) 85 7076
RATES: Seasonal: Dec. 18 - Apr. 19
  Single: $74.00 Double: $74.00 Extra: $10.00
RATES: Seasonal: Apr. 20 - Dec. 17
  Single: $58.00 Double: $58.00 Extra: $10.00
FACILITIES: Garage parking, 3 restaurants, convention facilities, gym, pool, sauna, tennis courts & much more to pamper your stay.

ACAPULCO, GRO., 39390, MEXICO   Motel
MOTEL LA JOLLA
Ave. Costera M. Aleman 506
  Tel: (74) 82 5858   FAX: Not listed
RATES: Yearly
  Single: $50.00 Double: $70.00 Extra: $7.00
FACILITIES: No pets, balconies, wading pool, restaurant nearby, refrigerators, shower baths, no T.V.

ACAPULCO, GRO., 39690, MEXICO   Economy
SANDS HOTEL
Ave. Costera M. Aleman 178
  Tel: (74) 84 2260 FAX: (74) 84 1053
RATES: Seasonal: Dec. 15 - Apr. 15
  Single: $58.00 Double: $58.00 Extra: $12.00
RATES: Seasonal: Apr. 16 - Dec. 14
  Single: $35.00 Double: $35.00 Extra: $12.00
FACILITIES: No pets. Central lawn and pool area, squash (fee), dining. coffee shop, cocktails, refrigerators, shower baths.

ACAYUCAN, VERA CRUZ, MEXICO   Inexpensive
3 HOTELS: LOS ANGELES, SAN MIGUEL AND RITZ
RATES: All three hotels are reasonable.
FACILITIES: Have fans, hot baths, pools, and TV. This town is the main turn off for Highway 185 if you are traveling down the East coast of Mexico and plan to cross the Isthmus to Tehuantepec and continue to the Guatemalan border. The Hotel Ritz has a place to camp with hookups.

CANCUN, Q.R. 77500, MEXICO   First Class
BEST WESTERN PLAZA CARIBE
Tulum Con Uxmal Lote 19 P.O. Box 487
  Tel: (98) 84 1377 FAX: (98) 84 6352
RATES: Seasonal: Dec. 15 - Apr. 15

Single: $85.00 Double: $85.00 Extra: $10.00
RATES: Seasonal: Apr. 16 - Dec. 14
Single: $55.00 Double: $55.00 Extra: $10.00
FACILITIES: Senior discount, No pets, pool playground, restaurant, coffee shop, cocktails, entertainment, valet laundry, free movies, safes, shower baths, cable T.V.

CANCUN, Q.R., 77500, MEXICO   First Class
CARROUSEL HOTEL
P.O. Box 407 Blvd. Kukulkan at Km 3.5 on the beach.
Tel: (98) 83 0388 FAX: (98) 83 2312
RATES: Yearly
Single: $90.00 Double: $90.00 Extra: $23.00
FACILITIES: No pets, ocean view, beach, pool, wading pool, whirlpool, tennis court (fee), 2 restaurants, free movies, shower baths, cable T.V., plus fee recreation.

**(RV) CHAPALA, JAL.,MEXICO   Economy
PAL TRAILER PARK
Between Chapala and Ajijic
Tel: 376/6-0040, 376/5-3764
RATES: **$5.00 per night**
FACILITIES: 106 sites, full hookups, heated pool , laundry,flush toilets and laundry.

CHIHUAHUA, CHIH., 31160, MEXICO   Motor Inn
HOTEL CASA GRANDE
Ave. Tecnológico 4702
Tel: (14) 19 6633 FAX: (19) 3235
RATES: Yearly
Single: $75.00 Double: $75.00 Extra: Request
FACILITIES: No pets, meeting rooms, pool, tennis court, restaurant, cocktails, free movies, cable T.V. Some room w/microwaves, refers.

CHIHUAHUA, CHIH., 31240, MEXICO   Motor Inn
MIRADOR MOTOR HOTEL
Ave. Universidad 1309 P.O. Box 827
Tel: (14) 13 2205 FAX: (14) 13 8906
RATES: Yearly
Single: $60.00 Double: $62.00 Extra: $4.00
FACILITIES: No pets, pool, wading pool, restaurant, coffee shop, free movies, shower baths, cable T.V.

CUERNAVACA, MOR., 62120, MEXICO   Motor Inn
HOSTERIA LAS QUINTAS
Ave. Las Quintas 107 P.0. Box 427
    Tel: (73) 18 3940 FAX: No listing
RATES: Yearly
    Single: $85.00 Double: $98.00 Extra: $20.00
FACILITIES: No pets, pool, whirlpool, dining room, refers, shower, bath, cable T.V.

DURANGO, DGO., 34000, MEXICO   Motor Inn
HOTEL GOBERNADOR
Ave. 20 de Noviembre 257
    Tel: (18) 13 1919 FAX: (18) 11 1422
RATES: Yearly
    Single: $91.00 Double: $91.00 Extra: $28.00
FACILITIES: No pets, meeting rooms, pool, wading pool, restaurant, cocktails, free movies, cable T.V.

DURANGO, DGO., 34240, MEXICO   Motor Inn
MOTEL LOS ARCOS
Heróico Colegio Militar 2204
    Tel: (18) 18 7777 FAX: (18) 18 7777
RATES: Yearly
    Single: $55.00 Double: $60.00 Extra: $5.00
FACILITIES: No pets, restaurant, cocktails, free movies, shower baths, cable T.V.

GUADALAJARA, JAL., 44100, MEXICO   First Class
BEST WESTERN HOTEL FENIX
Ave. Corona 160 P.0. Box 1-1151
    Tel: (36) 14 5714   FAX: (36) 13 4005
RATES: Yearly
    Single: $55.00 Double: $65.00 Extra: $5.00
FACILITIES: Senior discount, no pets, restaurant, cocktails, free movies, refrigerators, combo & shower baths, cable T.V.

GUADALAJARA, JAL., 44100, MEXICO   First Class
BEST WESTERN PLAZA GENOVA
Ave. Juarez 123
    Tel: (36) 13 7500 FAX: (36) 14 8253
RATES: Yearly
    Single: $60.00 Double: $65.00 Extra: $5.00
FACILITIES: No pets, meeting rooms, steam rooms, exercise room, din-

ing room, coffee shop, cocktails, entertainment, free movies, cable T.V., some rooms - whirlpool.

** (RV) GUADALAJARA, JAL., MEXICO   Economy
HACIENDA TRAILER PARK
P.O. Box 5-494, located 10 kn northwest of mexican Highway 15.
  Tel: 3/527-1724
RATES: $13.00 per night
FACILITIES: Full hookups, flush tiolets, heated pool and coin laundry.

** (RV) GUAYMAS, SON, MEXICO   Economy
PLAYA DE CORTES
P.O. Box 66, Guaymas, Son, Mexico. Located near main highway.
  Tel: 622/2-0135
RATES: $12.00
FACILITIES: 50 sites, pool, flush toilets and more.

GUAYMAS, SON., 85420, MEXICO   4 Star Hotel
ARMIDA HOTEL
Carr. Internacional Salida Norte
  Tel: (62) 24 3083 FAX: (62) 22 0448
RATES: Yearly
  Single: $40.00   Double: $40.00 Extra: $10.00
FACILITIES: Garage parking, all other fine services of a four star hotel.

GUAYMAS, SON., 85450, MEXICO   Motor Inn
HOTEL PLAYA DE CORTES
On Bacochilbampo Bay
  Tel: (62) 21 0135   FAX: (62) 22 0135
RATES: Yearly
  Single: $72.00 Double: $72.00 Extra: $8.00
FACILITIES: No pets, beach, pool, 2 tennis courts, 2 dining rooms, cocktails, shower and baths.

HERMOSILLO, SON   Mid-range
ENCANTO MOTEL
Blvd. Kino between Hotel Gánadara and the Araiza Inn.
  Tel: 62-14-47-30
RATES:
  About $50 all year
FACILITIES: Phone, TV and considered a good value.

** (RV) HERMOSILLO, SON, MEXICO   Inexpensive
Kino RV Park

East of the Hotel Fiesta Americana on Blvd. Kino.
Tel:62-15-31-97
RATES:
$12 per night A good bargain
FACILITIES: Hookups for your trailer or RV.

MAZATLAN, SIN., 82110, MEXICO   Motor Inn
AZTECA INN
Ave. Rodolfo T. Loaiza 307 P.0. Box 841
Tel: (69) 13 4655 FAX: (69) 13 7476
RATES: Yearly
Single: $24.00 Double: $30.00 Extra: $6.00
FACILITIES: No pets, beach, pool, whirlpool, restaurant, sidewalk cafe,
cocktail lounge, free movies, combo & shower baths, cable T.V.

MAZATLAN, SIN., 82000, MEXICO   Motor Inn
BEST WESTERN EL AGUA MARINA
Ave. del Mar 110
Tel: (69) 80 7080 FAX: (69) 82 4624
RATES: Yearly
Single: $60.00 Double: $60.00 Extra: $6.00
FACILITIES: Small pets only, beach, pool, wading pool, dining room,
cocktail lounge, free movies, combo & shower baths, cable T.V.

MAZATLAN, SIN., 82100, MEXICO   First Class
HOLIDAY INN MAZATLAN
Ave. Camarón Sabalos S/N 696
Tel: (69) 13 2222 FAX: (69) 14 1287
RATES: Seasonal: Dec. 15 - Apr. 15
Single: $60.00   Double: $60.00   Extra: $10.00
RATES: Seasonal: Apr. 16 - Dec. 14
Sgle: $45.00 Dble: $45.00 Xtra: $10.00
FACILITIES: No pets, meeting rooms, beach, pool, wading pool, res-
taurant, cocktail lounge, coffee makers, refrigerators, cable T.V.

MAZATLAN, SIN., 82110, MEXICO   Hotel Suites
HOTEL SUITES LAS FLORES
Ave. Rodolfo T. Loaiza 212 P.0. Box 583
Tel: (69) 13 5100 FAX: (69) 14 3422
RATES: Seasonal: Dec. 15 - Apr. 15
Single: $55.00 Double: $55.00 Extra: $10.00
RATES: Seasonal: Apr. 16 - Dec. 14
Sgle: $40.00 Dble: $40.00 Sgle: $7.00

FACILITIES: No pets, beach, pool, restaurant, coffee shop, free movies, combo & shower baths, cable T.V.

** (RV) MAZATLAN, SIN, MEXICO   Economy
LA POSTA TRAILER PARK There are about 10 other RV parks and campgrounds in this city. If this one is full ask for directions to one of the other locations.
Located near Cameron Glorieta
   Tel: 3-5310

MERIDA, YUC., 97000, MEXICO   First Class
DEL GOBERNADOR HOTEL
Calle 59 @ Calle 66 - 535 Calle 59
   Tel: (99) 23 7133 FAX: (99) 28 1590
RATES: Yearly
   Single: $55.00 Double: $55.00 Extra: $12.00
FACILITIES: No pets, meeting rooms, pool, dining room, restaurant, cocktail lounge, valet laundry, free movies, shower baths, cableT.V.

MERIDA, YUC., 97000, MEXICO   Economy
HOTEL CARIBE
Calle 59 - #500
   Tel: (99) 24 9022   FAX: (99) 24 8733
RATES: Yearly
   Sgle: $33.00 Dble: A39.00 Xtra: $4.00
FACILITIES: Senior discount, no pets, pool, (fee) golf & tennis, restaurant, coffee shop, shower baths.

MEXICO CITY, D.F., 06300, MEXICO   First Class
BEST WESTERN HOTEL MAJESTIC
Ave. Madero 73
   Tel: (55) 21 8609 FAX: (55) 12 6262
RATES: Yearly
   Single: $45.00 Double: $46.00 Extra: $10.00
FACILITIES: No pets, rooftop dining room, cocktails, valet laundry, free movies, safes.

MEXICO CITY D F. , 03810, MEXICO   Economy
HOTEL BEVERLY
301 New York Ave.
   Tel: (55) 23 6065   FAX: (56) 82 0751
RATES: Yearly
   Single: $38.00 Double: $50.00 Extra: S7.00

FACILITIES: No pets, restaurant, cocktails, valet parking, shower & tub baths.

MEXICO CITY, D.F., 06500, MEXICO — First Class
HOTEL DAYS INN MEXICO
Ave. Río Lerma 237
Tel: (52) 11 Ol09   FAX: (52) 08 2014
RATES: Yearly
Single: $85.00 Double: $90.00 Extra: $10.00
FACILITIES: No pets, restaurant, valet laundry, shower baths, cable T.V.

MEXICO CITY, D.F., 06500, MEXICO — First Class
HOTEL JARDIN AMAZONAS
Río Amazonas 73
Tel: (55) 33 5950 FAX: (55) 14 2440
RATES: Yearly
Single: $60.00 Double: $70.00 Extra: $18.00
FACILITIES: Pets, heated pool, restaurant, cocktails, valet laundry, shower baths, cable T.V.

MEXICO CITY, D.F., 06470, MEXICO — Economy
HOTEL MAYALAND
Antonio Caso #23, Col San Rafael
Tel: (52) 66 6066 FAX: (52) 35 1273
RATES: Yearly
Single: $30.00 Double: $33.00 Extra: $5.00
FACILITIES: Garage parking, restaurant, bar, room service, travel agency, FAX service, National & International phone service. We always stay here.

MEXICO CITY, D.F., 06700, MEXICO — Economy
HOTEL PARQUE ENSENADA
Ave. Alvaro Obregon 13
Tel: (52) 08 0052 FAX: (52) 08 0052
RATES: Yearly
Single: $59.00 Double: $65.00 Extra: $8.00
FACILITIES: No pets, restaurant, cocktails, free movies, safes, shower & tub baths, cableT.V.

MEXICO CITY, D.F., 06470, MEXICO — Economy
HOTEL PLAZA REFORMA
Ave. Insurgentes Centro 149

Tel: (52) 70 6111 FAX: (52) 66 7555
RATES: Yearly (1933)
　　Single: $60.00   Double: $70.00   Extra: $10.00
FACILITIES: Garage parking, restaurant & bar, terrace, carpeted rooms with tub, telephone, cable T.V., conference rooms.

MEXICO CITY, D.F., 06600, MEXICO　　　　First Class
HOTEL PRIM
Versalles #46, Col. Juarez
　　Tel: (52) 92 4600 FAX: (52) 92 4B35
RATES: Yearly (1993)
　　Single: $32.00 Double: $39.00 Extra: Request
FACILITIES: Garage parking, cafeteria, restaurant, piano bar, color T.V. phones, room service, laundry, safe deposit boxes.

MEXICO CITY, D.F., 06600, MEXICO　　　　Economy
HOTEL VIENA
Marsella 28
　　Tel: (55) 66 0700 FAX: (55) 92 7302
RATES: Yearly
　　Single: $40.00 Double: $48.00 Extra: $3.00
FACILITIES: No pets, Dining room, cocktails, valet laundry, combo shower & baths.

MEXICO CITY, D.F., 06600, MEXICO　　　Apartment Hotel
SUITES MI CASA
General Prim l06
　　Tel: (55) 66 6711   FAX: (55) 66 6010
RATES: Yearly
　　Single: $55.00 Double: $65.00 Extra: $10.00
FACILITIES: No pets, fully equipped with kitchen, restaurant nearby, valet laundry, refrigerators, shower baths.

MONTERREY, N.L., 66450, MEXICO　　　　Motor Inn
BEST WESTERN ROYAL COURTS
Ave. Universidad 314
　　Tel: (83) 76 2292 FAX: Not listed.
RATES: Yearly
　　Single:$73.00 Double: $82.00 Extra: $10.00
FACILITIES: No pets, secure parking, heated pool, restaurant, cocktails, valet laundry, free movies, shower baths, cable T.V.

MONTERREY, N.L., 64310, MEXICO   Motel
HOLIDAY INN EXPRESS
Ave. Eugenio Garza Sada 36
   Tel: (83) 29 6000 FAX: (83) 29 6020
RATES: Mon - Thurs.
   Single: $94.00 Double: $94.00 Extra $10.00
RATES: Fri. - Sun.
   Sgle: $71.00 Dble: $71.00 Xtra: $10.00
FACILITIES: Senior discount, no pets, heated pool, restaurant nearby, valet laundry, free movies, cable T.V.

** (RV) OAXACA,OAX, MEXICO   Economy
OAXACA TRAILER PARK
P.O. Box 33, Oaxaca, Oaxaca, Mexico. About a mile from Highway 190.
   Tel: 951/5-2796
RATES: $10.00
FACILITIES: Full hookups, around 150 sites, pool, laundry, flush tiolets and laundry.

OAXACA, OAX., 68000, MEXICO   First Class
HOTEL FORTIN PLAZA
Ave. Venus 118
   Tel: (95) 15 7777 FAX: (95) 15 1328
RATES: Yearly
   Single: $65.00 Double: $75.00 Extra: $10.00
FACILITIES: No pets, pool, restaurant, cocktails, valet laundry, free movies, shower baths, cable T.V.

OAXACA, OAX., 68000, MEXICO   Economy
HOTEL SENORIAL
Portal de Flores 6 - Facing Zócalo
   Tel: (95) 16 3933 FAX: (95) 16 3668
RATES: Yearly
   Single: $35.00 Double: $45.00 Extra: $6.00
FACILITIES: No pets, pool, fee parking, dining room, cocktails, valet laundry, shower baths.

OAXACA, OAX., 68000, MEXICO   Luxury
PRESIDENTE OAXACA
5 de Mayo 300
   Tel: (95) 16 0609 FAX: (95) 16 0732
RATES: Yearly
   Single: $130.00 Double: $130.00 Extra: $20.00

FACILITIES: Senior discount, no pets, heated pool, dining room, cocktails, valet laundry, free movies, cable T.V.

PUERTO ESCONDIDO, OAX., 71980, MEXICO   Motor Inn
HOTEL FIESTA MEXICANA
Blvd. Benito Juarez
    Tel: (95) 82 0115 FAX: (95) 82 0115
RATES: Yearly
    Single: $50.00 Double: $50.00 Extra: $10.00
FACILITIES: No pets, 3 pools, wading pool, lighted tennis court, transportation to beach, 3 restaurants, nightclub, shower baths, cable T.V.

** (RV) PUERTO ESCONDIDO, OAX, MEXICO   Economy
PUERTO ESCONDIDO TRAILER PARK
Avenida Alfonso Perez Gazga. Located 1.5 km west of Hwy. 200
    Tel: 958/2-0077
RATES: $8.00 per day
FACILITIES: Showers, pool, toilets, and laundry.

PUERTO ESCONDIDO, OAX., 71980, MEXICO   Country Inn
HOTEL SANTA FE
Calle del Morro at south end of town.
    Tel: (95) 82 0170 FAX: (95) 82 0260
RATES: Yearly
    Single: $49.00 Double: $59.00 Extra: $8.00
FACILITIES: No pets, pool, wading pool, restaurant, cocktails, valet laundry, shower baths, black & white T.V.

** (RV) PUERTO VALLARTA, JAL, MEXICO   Economy
LAURIES "TACHO" TRAILER PARK
P.O. Box 315, Puerto Vallarta, Jal., Mexico. Located 6.3 km on Mexican Highway 200 and 1 km east.
    Tel: 3224-2163
RATES: $10.00 to $12.00
FACILITIES: Full hookups, pool and laundry.

PUERTO VALLARTA, JAL., 48310, MEXICO   Luxury
HACIENDA BUENAVENTURA
Ave. Mexico 200 P.O. Box 95B
    Tel: (32) 22 3737 FAX: (32) 24 6400
RATES: Seasonal: Dec. 19 - Apr. 16
    Single: $40.00 Double: $50.00 Extra: $10.00
RATES: Seasonal: Apr. 17 - Dec. 18

Single: $30.00 Double: $34.00 Extra: $6.00
FACILITIES: No pets, beach, pool, wading pool, 2 restaurants, cocktails, free movies, combo & shower bath - some refers extra.

PUERTO VALLARTA, JAL., 48310, MEXICO Motor Inn
HOTEL PELICANOS
Francisco Medina Ascencio
Tel: (32) 24 1010 FAX: (32) 24 1111
RATES: Seasonal: Dec. 16 - Apr. 19
Single: $70.00 Double: $70.00 Extra: Request
RATES: Seasonal: Apr. 20 - Dec. 15
Single: $50.00 Double: $50.00 Extra: Request
FACILITIES: No pets, beach, 3 pools, restaurant, cocktails, all rooms, shower baths, some rooms cable T.V.

PUERTO VALLARTA, JAL., 48300, MEXICO Motor Inn
LAS PALMAS BEACH RESORT
Blvd. Francisco tledina Ascencio P.0. Box 55
Tel: (32) 24 0650 FAX: (32) 24 0543
RATES: Seasonal: Dec. 20 - Apr. 15
Single: $65.00 Double: $75.00 Extra: $10.00
RATES: Seasonal: Apr. 16 - Dec. 19
Single: $45.00 Double: $55.00 Extra: $10.00
FACILITIES: No pets, beach, pool, wading pool, restaurant, cocktails, shower baths, cable T.V.

PUERTO VALLARTA, JAL., 48380, MEXICO Deluxe
SUITES MEZA DEL MAR
Amapas #380
Tel: (32) 22 4888 FAX: (32) 22 2308
RATES: Seasonal: Dec. 1 - Apr. 15
Single: $67.00 Double: $67.00 Extra: $25.00
RATES: Seasonal: Apr. 16 - Nov. 30
Single: $65.00 Double: $65.00 Extra: $25.00
FACILITIES: Senior discount, no pets, 1 to 3 bedroom apartments with full kitchen, beach, 2 pools, wading pool, tennis court, restaurant, deli, cocktails, shower baths, somewith refrigerators, telephones.

QUERETARO, QRO., 76010, MEXICO Economy
HOTEL EMPERADOR
Prol. Corregidora Sur #240
Tel: (42) 13 2335   FAX: (42) 13 2395
RATES: Yearly

Single: $25.00 Double: $30.00 Extra: $8.00
FACILITIES: No pets, pool, restaurant, valet laundry, free movies, shower baths, cableT.V.

QUERETARO, QRO., 76140, MEXICO   Motor Inn
HOTEL REAL DE MINAS
Libre Celaya Hwy
  Tel: (42) 16 0444 FAX: (42) 16 0662
RATES: Yearly
  Single: $80.00 Double: $80.00 To 4 persons.
FACILITIES: No pets, golf privileges, heated pool, wading pool, 7 tennis courts, playground, restaurant, coffee shop, cocktails, valet laundry, free movies, combo & shower baths, cable T.V.

SALTILLO, COAH., 25260, MEXICO   Motor Inn
BEST WESTERN EUROTEL PLAZA
America Latina & Blvd. V.C.
  Tel: (84) 15 1000   FAX: No listing
RATES: Yearly
  Single: $63.00 Double: $66.00 Extra: $6.00
FACILITIES: No pets, lighted tennis court, playground, dining room, coffee shop, golf course privileges, 2 pools, valet laundry, free movies, Cable T.V.

SALTILLO, COAH., 25000, MEXICO   First Class
HOTEL SAN JORGE
Manuel Acuña 240 NTE
  Tel: (84) 12 2222 FAX: No listing
RATES: Yearly
  Single: $32.00 Double: $40.00 Extra: $6.00
FACILITIES: No pets, heated rooftop pool, dining room, rooftop restaurant, cocktails, free movies, combo & shower baths, Cable T.V.

SAN LUIS POTOSI, S.L.P., 78070, MEXICO   Motor Inn
CACTUS MOTEL
P.O. Box 393 On Mex 57, 1 Km SE of Gloria Juárez
  Tel: (48) 22 1995 FAX: (48) 14 4259
RATES: Yearly
  Single: $48.00 Doubl: $48.00 Extra: $5.00
FACILITIES: No pets, pool, playground, restaurant, cocktails, nightclub, free movies, combo & shower baths, cableT.V.

SAN LUIS POTOSI,S.L.P., 78210, MEXICO
BEST WESTERN HOTEL TUNA   Motor Inn
Ave. Dr. Manuel Nava #200
   Tel: (48) 13 1207 FAX: (48) 11 1415
RATES: Yearly
   Single: $45.00 Double: $55.00 Extra: $10.00
FACILITIES: No pets, garage parking, satellite T.V., swimming pool, restaurant & bar, shower baths.

** (RV) SAN LUIS POTOSI, S.L.P., MEXICO   Economy
CACTUS MOTOR TAILER PARK
P.O. Box 393, San Luís Potosí, S.L.P., Mexico 78770. On highway 57.
   Tel: 2-01871
RATES: $15.00 per day
FACILITIES: Pool and more.

SAN LUIS POTOSI, S.L.P., MEXICO   Motor Inn
HOTEL REAL DE MINAS
On Mex. 57, 1 Km. SE of G Juárez P.O. Box F-1371
   Tel: (48) 18 2616 FAX: (48) 18 6915
RATES: Yearly
   Single: $76.00 Double: $88.00 Extra: $10.00
FACILITIES: No pets, heated pool, lighted tennis court, restaurant, cafeteria, nightclub, free movies, combo shower & bath, and cable T.V.

SAN LUIS POTOSI, S.L.P., 78250, MEXICO   First Class
HOTEL REAL PLAZA
On Mex. 80, Ave. Carranza 890
   Tel: (48) 14 6055 FAX: (48) 14 6639
RATES::Yearly
   Single: $60.00 Double: $70.00 Exrta: $8.00
FACILITIES: No pets, luxury level rooms, pool, restaurant, coffee shop, nightclub, free movies and cable T.V.

TAMPICO, VER., 89300, MEXICO   Motor Inn
CAMINO REAL MOTOR HOTEL
Ave. Hidalgo 2000
   Tel: (12) 13 8811 FAX: (12)13 9226
RATES: Yearly
   Single: $115.00 Double: $115.00 Extra: $12.00
FACILITIES: No pets, tennis & golf privileges, pool, playground, dining room, coffee shop, valet laundry, free movies and cable T.V.

TAPACHULA,CHIS., MEXICO　　　**Mid-range to inexpensive**
3 HOTELS: MOTEL LOMA REAL (1st classs),
Tel;: 61440; FENIX Tel: 50755; DON MIGUEL Tel: 61143
This town is near the border with Guatemala. Many tarvelers spend
the night here to get an early start before entering Guatemala. **(RV)
facilities at the **Autocinema Trailer Park**.

TEHUANTEPEC, MEXICO　　　**Mid-range**
HOTELS: POSADA DEL ISTMO AND OASIS (downtown)
** **RV PARK: SANTA TERESA TRAILER PARK**. Located to the east
of town, 8 km off Route 190. $6.00 per night, showers, and restaurant.

TEPIC, NAY., 63130, MEXICO　　　**Motor Inn**
MOTEL LA LOMA
Paseo de La Loma 301
　　Tel: (32) 13 2222 FAX: Not listed
RATES: Yearly
　　Single: $40.00 Double: $52.00 Extra: $10.00
FACILITIES: No pets, pool, wading pool, restaurant, cocktails, shower
& tub, restaurant, and cable T.V.

VERA CRUZ, VER., 94290, MEXICO　　　**Suites**
HOTEL SUITES MEDITERRANEO
Blvd. M. Aleman, Carr. Mocambo/Boca del Río
　　Tel: (29) 86 0323 FAX: (29) 31 0330
RATES: Yearly
　　Single. $30.00 Double: $35.00 Extra: $7.00
FACILITIES: No pets, secure parkng, breakfast, bar, service bar, pool,
beach, A/C and showers.

**** (RV) VERACRUZ, VER., MEXICO**　　　**Economy**
PARADOR LOS ARCOS
8 km south on Highway 180
　　Tel: 37-40-75
RATES: $8.00
FACILITIES: 100 spaces and more.

VILLAHERMOSA, TAB., 86050, MEXICO　　　**Motor Inn**
CALDINA VIVA VILLAHERMOSA
1.5 Km. N on Mex. 180
　　Tel: (93) 15 0000 FAX: (93) 15 3073
RATES: Yearly
　　Single: $83.00 Double: $83.00 Extra: $10.00

FACILITIES: No pets, pool, wading pool, restaurant, nightclub, valet laundry, free movies, shower baths and cable T.V.

GUATEMALA HOTEL AND
MOTEL RATES

GUATEMALA CITY, 01001 GUATEMALA   First Class
POSADA BELEN HOTEL & TRAVEL
13 Calle "A" 10-30, Zona 1
   Tel: (502) 253 4530 FAX: (502) 251 3478
RATES: Yearly - 1996
   Single: $36.00 Double: $43.00 Extra: $8.00
FACILITIES: Colonial style house, secure parking, private bath, hot water, centrally located, safe deposit boxes, fan, laundry services, garage next door, English spoken, restaurant, tours, travel info., Fax service,and storage.

GUATEMALA CITY, GUATEMALA   Economy
HOTEL EXCELL
"A" Ave. 15-12, Zona 1
   Tel: (502) 253 2769 FAX: None
RATES: Yearly - 1995
   Single: $15.00 Double: $18.00 Extra: $4.00
FACILITIES: Garage parking, restaurant, TV in every room, private bathrooms in every room.

GUATEMALA CITY, GUATEMALA   Luxury
HOTEL RITZ CONTINENTAL
6A Avenida "A" 10-13, Zona 1
   Tel: (502) 2-82513 FAX: (502) 2-81527
RATES: Yearly - 1996 - Silver Tower
   Single: $70.00 Double: $75.00 Extra: $10.00
RATES: Yearly - 1996 - Golden Tower
   Single: $90.00 Double: $95.00 Extra: $10.00
FACILITIES: Garage parking, located in heart of downtown near National Palace, restaurants & bars, heated pool and car rental.

BELIZE HOTEL
AND MOTEL RATES

BELIZE CITY, BELIZE   Mid-range

MOPAN HOTEL
(Consult other Central American Travel guides for more listings)
55 Regent St.
Tel: (2) 77351/73356 FAX: 75383
RATES:
Single: $21.00 Double: $32.00 airconditioning extra

FACILITIES: Nice ambience. good bar for meeting other travelers.
Satellite TV.

BENQUE VIEJO DEL CARMEN, BELIZE   Mid-range
HOTEL MAYA
(Consult other Central American travel giudes for additonal listings)
11 George St.
Tel: 093-2116
RATES: Expensive.
FACILITIES: This towlast city on the Belize side and one mile from
the border.. Basic accomodattions inall of the hotels here.. If you are
going on to Guatemala the hotels on the Guatemalan side are
cheaper.

EL SALVADOR HOTEL AND
MOTEL RATES

SAN SALVADOR, EL SALVADOR, C. A.   Economy
HOTEL VISTALAGO,
12 Carretera a Apulo, Ilopango
Tel: (503) 295 0532 FAX: None listed
RATES: Yearly - 1996
Single: $25.00 Double: $25.00 Xtra: $5.00
FACILITIES: Restaurant, bar, indoor parking, parking for campers, lake
nearby.

SAN SALVADOR, EL SALVADOR, C.A.   First Class
HOTEL EL SALVADOR
89 Avenida Norte y 11 Calle Poniente, Col. Escalón
Tel: (503) 79 0777 FAX: (503) 79 3913
RATES: Yearly - 1994
Single: $75.00 Double: $75.00 Extra: $10.00
FACILITIES: Secure parking, 200 room, telephone, air conditioned, color
TV, coffee shop, pool, tennis & racquet club, located in one of the best
residential areas.

SAN SALVADOR, EL SALVADOR, C. A.   Luxury
HOTEL PRESIDENTE
Final Ave La Revolucion, Col. San Benito P.0.288 Tel: (503) 79 4444
FAX:(503) 23 4912
RATES: Yearly - 1994
 Single: $91.00 Double: $91.00 Extra: $10.00
FACILITIES: Garage parking, restaurant, laundry, dry cleaning, 24 Hr.
room service, bar, discotheque, outdoor pools—one for children & one
for adults, gym, sauna, massage, futbol, basketball, volley ball areas.

SAN SALVADOR, EL SALVADOR, C. A.   First Class
RAMADA INN
Colonia Escalón - 85 Av. Sur y Calle J.J.Canas
 Tel: (503) 279 1700 FAX: (503) 279 1889
RATES: Yearly - 1996
 Single: $59.00 Double: $67.00 Extra: $12.00
FACILITIES: Bar, restaurant, swimming pool, three reception areas 150
- 200 persons, two fully equipped conference rooms, dry cleaning, fax
service, International phone service.

SAN SALVADOR, EL SALVADOR, C.A.   First Class
HOTEL SIESTA
Autopista sur @ Basilica de Guadelupe/APOO 01217
 Tel: (503) 79 0377 FAX: (503) 24 6575
RATES: Yearly - 1994
 Single: $64.00 Double: $71.00 Extra: $9.00
FACILITIES: Garage parking, swimming pool, air conditioning, cable
TV, carpeted rooms.

HONDURAS HOTEL AND
MOTEL RATES

CHOLUTECA, HONDURAS, C. A.   First Class
HOTEL CAMINO REAL
Salida a Guasaule
 Tel: (504) 82 0630 FAX: (504) 82 2860
RATES: yearly - 1994
 Single: $18.00 Double: $20.00 Extra: Request
 Cottage for 4 persons: $27.00
FACILITIES: Secure parking, restaurant, swimming pool .

CHOLUTECA, HONDURAS, C.A.   First Class
HOTEL LA FUENTE

Pan-American Highway
Tel: (504) 82 0263 FAX: (504) 82 0273
RATES: Yearly - 1994
Single: $30.00 Double: $35.00 Extra: $5.00
FACILITIES: Secure parking, restaurant, bar, swimming pool,laundry services, banquet and meeting room facilities for 200 capacity, TV, international Fax and telephone service.

SAN PEDRO SULA, CORTES, HONDURAS   **First Class**
GRAN HOTEL SULA
Calle 1 & Ave. 4 - P.O.Box 435
Tel: (504) 52 9999 FAX: (504) 52 7000
FACILITIES: Secure parking, dining room, 24 Hr. service in Cafeteria.

TEGUCIGALPA, HONDURAS, C. A.   **First Class**
ALAMEDA HOTEL
Blvd. Suyapa - P.O. Box 940
Tel: (504) 32 6920 FAX: (504) 32 6932
RATES: Yearly - 1994
Single: $55.00 Double: $65.00 Extra: $10.00
FACILITIES: Secure parking, 75 luxurious rooms, color TV, air conditioning, Beauty Rest mattresses, swimming pool, snack bar, beverage service, sauna, massage, restaurant, bar, conference room. Honors all major credit cards.

TEGUCIGALPA, HONDURAS, C.A.   **First Class**
HOTEL HONDURAS MAYA
Ave. República de Chile, Col. Palmera
Tel: (504) 32 3191 FAX: (504) 32 7629
RATES: Yearly - 1996
Single: $124.00 Double: $137.00 Extra: $13.00
FACILITIES: Secure parking, restaurant, bar, conference rooms, swimming pool, color TV, telephones, beauty shop, souvenirs, convention facilities.

TEGUCIGALPA, HONDURAS, C.A.   **Luxury**
HOTEL PLAZA SAN MARTIN
Colonial Palmira, Front of Plaza San Martín
Tel: (504) 37 2928 FAX: (504) 31 1366
RATES: Yearly - 1996
Single: $102.50 Double: $122.50 Extra: $25.00
FACILITIES: Garage parking, spacious rooms, air conditioning, two double beds, terrace with panoramic view of city and mountains, restaurant and lobby bar, secretarial services.

TEGUCIGALPA, HONDURAS, C.A.   First Class
HOTEL PRADO
Ave. Cervantes opposite the Cathedral
    Tel: (504) 37 0121 FAX: (504) 37 2221
RATES: Yearly - 1995
    Single: $54.00 Double: $65.00 Extra: $9.00
    Suite: $76.00 Jr. Suite: $65.00
FACILITIES: Secure parking, cafeteria, bar, conference rooms, cable TV, telephones, and air conditioning,.

NICARAGUA HOTEL AND
MOTEL RATES

GRANADA, NICARAGUA, C.A.   Economy
HOTEL ALHAMBRA
West side, Central Park
    Tel: (552) 4485 FAX: (552) 2035
RATES: Yearly - 1996
    Single: $31.00 Double: $35.00 Extra: $8.00
FACILITIES: Bar, restaurant, cafeteria, pool, cable T.V., conference rooms and tour guide.

LEON, NICARAGUA, C.A.   Economy
HOTEL AMERICA
Mercado Central 1 block east.
    Tel: (505) 0311 (505) FAX: Not listed.
RATES: Yearly - 1996
    Single: $7.00 Double: $15.00 Extra: $5.00
FACILITIES: Garage near hotel, restaurant, telephone service, located in center of city.

MANAGUA, NICARAGUA   Economy
HOTEL ESTRELLA
Semáforos de Rubenia 400 Yds North, P.O.Box 795
    Tel: (505) 97 010 FAX: (505) 29 7104
RATES: Yearly - 1994
    Single: $27.50 Double: $36.00 Extra: $9.00
FACILITIES: Garage parking, dining room, bar, conference room, air conditioning, telephone, swimming pool, and cable TV.

MANAGUA, NICARAGUA, C.A.   First Class
HOTEL LAS MERCEDES
Carretera norte acroos from the airport

Tel :(505) 63 1011 FAX: (505-) 631082
RATES: Yearly - 1995
    Single: $60.00 Double: $65.00 Extra: $10.00
FACILITIES: Parking, restaurant, bar, room service, barber at beauty shop, gift shop, 2 swimming pools, 2 tennis courts, convention and banquet facilities,
FAX & Phone service.

MANAGUA, NICARAGUA, C.A.   Luxury
HOTEL TICOMO
Km. 8.5 de La Carr. Sur.
RATES: Yearly - 1994
    Single: $40.00 Double: $60.00 Extra: $5.00
FACII ITIES: Secure garage, kitchen, refrigerator.

MATAGALPA, NICARAGUA, C.A.   Luxury Bungalows
SELVA NEGRA MOUNTAIN RESORT
Km 140 Carr. Mataqalpa - Junotega
    Tel: (505) 61 23883 FAX: (505) 61 22554
RATES: Yearly - 1996
    Single: $15.00 Double: $30.00-$50.00 Extra: $15.00
FACILITIES: Bar, International restaurant, hiking horseback riding, youth hostel, parking facilities, room service.

COSTA RICA HOTEL AND
MOTEL RATES

CALDERA, PUNTARENAS, COSTA RICA, C.A.   First Class
HOTEL DUNDEE RANCH
57 Km from International Airport, So. of Caldera
    Tel: (506) 48 8775 FAX: (506) 39 7050
RATES: Yearly - 1994
    Single: 76.00 Double: $76.00 Extra: $10.00
FACILITIES: Secure parking, dining room, Continental or American breakfast, bar, 1 swimming pool for kids - 1 for adults, horseback riding and walking trails.

CIUDAD CARIARI, COSTA RICA, C.A.   Luxury
VISTA DE GOLF
La Marina APDO 379-4005, San Antonio de Belén
    Tel: (506) 239 4348 FAX: (506) 255 3238
RATES: High Season -Dec/Apr plus July

Single: $70.00 Double: $70.00 Extra: $10.00
FACILITIES: 24 hour security parking, fruit Continental breakfasts, direct dial telephones, color T.V., suites with equipped kitchens, cutlery and glassware for 5 persons, swimming pool & spa, B.B.Q. and weekly buffets, potable water, photocopy and fax, ventilation fans in every room, arrangements for golf and horseback riding.

HEREDIA, SAN RAFAEL, COSTA RICA, C.A.　　　First Class
HOTEL TIROL
Monte de la Cruz, San Rafael de Heredia
　　Tel: (506) 39 1371 FAX: (506) 30 7050
RATES: Yearly - 1995
　　Single: $80.00 Double: $80.00/$155.00 Extra: $10.00
FACILITIES: Secure parking, dining room, tennis courts, 2 meeting roorns, horseback riding, walking trails in our private reserve in a rain cloud forest.

HEREDIA, COSTA RICA, C.A.　　　Mountain Resort
HOTEL EL PORTICO
San Joseé de la Montaña above Barva
　　Tel: (506) 260 6000 FAX: (506) 260 6002
RATES: Dec. 1, l996- Apr. 30, 1996
　　Single $35.00 Double: $70.00 Extra: $10.00
RATES: May 1, 1996 - Nov. 30, 1996
　　Single: $35.00 Double: $45.00 Extra: $10.00
FACILITIES: Bar, restaurant, garage parsing, room service, fireplaces, swimming pool, sauna, jacuzzi, conference rooms, satellite T.V. and VHS., international phones.

HEREDIA, COSTA RICA, C.A.　　　First Class
VALLADOLID HOTEL
Ave. 7, Calle 7 - Apartado 93-3000
　　Tel: (.505) 260 2905 FAX: (506) 260 2912
RATES: Yearly - l99
　　Single: $56.00 Double: $60.00 Extra: $15.00
　　Suite for 2 persons: $64.00 - $72.80
FACILITIES: Secure parking, refrigerators in all rooms, microwave, color cable TV, hair dryer, air conditioning, hot water, tub a shower in suites, telepnones, plus panoramic view bar, jacuzzi, sauna and gourmet restaurant, travel agency, roon service, secretarial, legal, and medical aid.

LIBERIA, GUANACASTE, COSTA RICA, C.A.   Economy
HOTEL GUANACASTE TRAVEL LODGE
Call 12 & Ave. 1 P.0. Box 251-5000
   Tel: (506) 66 0085 FAX: (506) 66 0085
RATES: Yearly - 1996
   Single: $16.00 Double: .$14.00 Extra: $5.00
FACILITIES: Ample parking, trailer park, rent-a-car, restaurant, bar,
free tours.

LIMON, COSTA RICA, C.A.   First Class
HOTEL MARIBU CARIBE
APDO. 625 - 7300
   Tel::(506) 58 4010 FAX: (506) 58 3541
RATES: Seasonal - 15 may 1992 - 15 Sept. 1992
   Single: $46.00 Double: $55.00 Extra: $ 10.00
RATES: Seasonal - 16 Sept. 1992 - 15 Sept. 1993
   Single: $65.00 Double: $75.00 XExra: $10.00
FACILITIES: Secure parking, dinning room, dinning service, tele-
phones, swimming pool, snack bar, air conditioned, U.S. dollars and
travelers checks accepted.

MANUEL ANTONIO, QUEPOS, COSTA RICA, C.A.   First Class
HOTEL ARBOLEDA
Manuel Antonio/Quepos - P.O. Box 55 - 6350
   Tel: (506) 777 1056 FAX: 777 0092
RATES: Seasonal - May - November, 1996
   Single; $65.00 Double: $75.00 Exra: $10.00
RATES: Seasonal - May - November, 1996
   Single: $40.00 Double: $50.00 Extra: 10.00
FACILITIES: Beachfront, air conditioned, pool parking, surfing, fish-
ing, 2 restaurants, gift shop, squash and spa.

MANUEL ANTONIO,QUEPOS, COSTA RICA,C.A.   Mid-range
HOTEL PLINIO
Apdo. 71, Quepos
   Tel: (506) 777-0055 FAX: (506) 777-0558
RATES:
   $50.00 daily, $60.00 with airconditioning
   $75.00 for a two-story suite
FACILITIES: Tropical ambience,nearby jungle trails, 14 rooms, hot
water, restaurant and bar.

**RV)SAN ANTONIO DE BELEN, COSTA RICA   Economy
BELEN TRAILER PARK
Tel: (506) 239-0421 FAX: (506) 239-1316
RATES: $6.50 per for camping, $ 8.50 per night RV
FACILITIES: Fully equipped Rv and Campsite, hook-ups for RV, electricity, water, showers,and washing machines.

SAN JOSE, COSTA RICA, C.A.   First Class
HOTEL DEL REY
Avenida 1, Calle 9, one block south of Morazán Park
Tel: (506) 221-7272 FAX: (506) 221-0096
RATES:
Single: $39.00-$75.00 Double: $68.00-$75.00 Suites: $125.00
FACILITIES: Thsi place is the *gringo* hangout in San José. Convient downtown location, 104 rooms, suites with living room and balconies, full-service tour agency, "Richard Krug" resident sportfishing expert, 24-hour restaurant, free guided city tour, casino, and the great Blue Marlin Bar where your can watch sporting events on cable TV, hear some tall fish tales and check out the local beauties.

SAN JOSE, COSTA RICA, C.A.   First Class
HOTEL AMBASSADOR
Avenida Central between Calle 26 and 28
Tel: (506) 221 8155 FAX: (506) 255 3396
RATES: Yearly - 1995
Single: $45.00 Double: $55.00 Extra: $10.00
FACILITIES: Secure parking, dining room, cable T.V., restaurant, bar and telephones.

SAN JOSE, COSTA RICA, C.A.   Apartotel
APARTOTEL SABANA
Tel: (506) 296 0276 FAX: (506) 231 7386
RATES: Seasonal - Dec 1, 1995 - Apr 30, 1996
Single: $45.00 Double: $45.00-$90.00 Plus Tax
RATES: Seasonal - May 1, 1996 - Nov. 30, 1996
Single: $40.00-$80.00 Double: $40.00-$90.00 Plus Tax
FACILITIES: Queen-size bed, breakfast bar, fully equipped kitchens, saunas, pools, security service, laundry service, coin-op laundry.

**SAN JOSE, COSTA RICA, C.A.   Economy
DUNN INN
Calle 5, Avenida 9
Tel: (506) 222-3232 FAX: (506) 221-4596

RATES:

From $45.00 with the seventh night free.

FACILITIES: A renowned *gringo* hangout, nice quaint atmosphere in a restored Spanish-colonial home, cable TV and phones, patio restaurant with ferns, centrally located and very good service. We recommend it highly.

SAN JOSE, COSTA RICA, C.A.   Economy
HOTEL MUSOC
Calle 16 between Avenida 1 and 3

Tel: (506) 222 9437 FAX: (506) 233 2643

RATES: Yearly - 1994

Single: $10.00 Double: $16.00 Extra: $5.00

FACILITIES: Secure garage, cafeteria and restaurant, laundry, shuttle service between airport and hotel, safe deposit boxes, hot water, cable T.V. in lobby.

SAN JOSE COSTA RICA, C. A.   Economy
HOTEL PLAZA
Avenida Central between Calles 2 and 4

Tel: (506) 257 1896 FAX: (506) 222 2641

RATES: Yearly - 1996

Single: $31.00 Double: $39.00 Extra: $11.00

FACILITIES: Centrally located, bar, restaurant, remote control color T.V., private baths, room service, parking and laundry facilities.

SAN JOSE, COSTA RICA, C. A.   Economy
SAN JOSE GARDEN COURT HOTEL
7th Ave and Calle 6 - P. O. Box 1849-1002

Tel: (506) 255 4766 FAX: (506) 255 4613

RATES: Yearly - 1996

Single: $34.99 Double: $47.50 Extra: $6.00

FACILITIES: Secure garage, dining room, includes American Breakfast, tour desk, swimming pool, air conditioned, cable T.V., telephone and a full-bath in each roorn.

SAN JOSE, COSTA RICA, C.A.   First Class
HOTEL VILLA TOURNON
Apartado 6606 - 1000

Tel: (506) 233 6622 FAX: 222 5211

RATES: Yearly - 1996

Single: $64.00 Double: $469.00 Extra: Request

FACILITIES: Free underground parking, dining room, bar, swimming pool, jacuzzi, money exchange, tour desk, lush landscaped grounds, yet walking distance downtown. Every detail of this eighty -room hotel is supervised for your comfort and personal service.

PANAMA HOTEL
RATES

PANAMA, REPUBLIC OF PANAMA, C.A   **Suites**
TOWER HOUSE SUITES
Calle 51 Bella Vista, P.0. Box 55 0309
   Tel: (507) 69 2244 FAX: (507) 269 2869
RATES: Yearly - 1996
   Single: $35.00 Double: $40.00 Extra: $5.00
FACILITIES: Secure garage parking, gym, swimming pool, conference room, laundry, room service from restaurants in the area. Each suite has lounge, cable TV and kitchenette.

PANAMA, REPUBLIC OF PANAMA, C.A.   **Moderate**
HOTEL CALIFORNIA
Vía España at Calle 43
   Tel: (507) 63 7844
FACILITIES: Air-conditioning, TV, hot water, private bath, bar, restaurant and good security.

PANAMA, REPUBLIC OF PANAMA, C.A.   **Moderate**
EL EJECUTIVO
Calle Aquilino de la Guardia
   Tel: (507) 64 3333 FAX: (507) 69 1944
FACILITIES: Pool, restaurant, private baths and showers, good security and excellent views. We always stay at this hotel when in Panama.

PANAMA, REPUBLIC OF PANAMA,C.A.   **Moderate**
HOTEL MONREAL
Vía España at AVE. Justo Aresemena
   Tel: (507) 63 4422
FACILITIES: Air-conditioning, private baths, hot water, color T.V. and phone.

NOTE: ** (RV) = RV facilities and sometimes campgrounds.

METRIC CONVERSIONS

To Convert	Multiply By	To Find
LENGTH		
Inches	2.54	Centimeters
Feet	30.0	Centimeters
Yards	0.9	Meters
Miles	1.6	Kilometers
Centimeters	0.4	Feet
Meters	3.3	Yards
Kilometers	0.62	Miles
VOLUME		
Teaspoon	5.0	Milliliters
Tablespoon	0.45	Milliliters
Fluid Ounces	30.0	Milliliters
Cups	0.24	Liters
Pints	0.47	Liters
Quarts	0.95	Liters
Gallons (U.S.)	3.8	Liters
Gallons (Imp.)	4.5	Liters
Liters	2.1	Pints
Liters	1.06	Quarts
Liters	0.26	Gallons (U.S.)
Liters	0.22	Gallons (Imp.)
WEIGHT		
Ounces	28.0	Grams
Pounds	0.45	Kilograms
Grams	0.035	Ounce
Kilograms	2.2	Pounds

TEMPERATURE
°Centigrade = (°F - 32) times .555
°Fahrenheit = (°C x 1.8) plus 32.0

To Convert	To	Multiply By
Centimeter	Inches	0.3937
Grams	Ounces	0.03527
Hectares	Acres	2.471
Kilograms	Pounds	2.205
Kilometers	Miles	0.6214
Liters	Gallons	0.2642
Liters	Pints	2.113
Meters	Feet	3.281
Meters	Yards	1.094
Square km	Acres	247.1
Square km	Sq. Miles	0.3861
Centigrade	Fahrenheit	1.8 then add 32

QUESTIONNAIRE

Dear reader: To help us with our next year's edition, please fill out this questionnaire and send it to one of the addresses listed below. You will be given mention for your efforts. We thank you for using this guidebooks and hope it has been of help to you.

Costa Rica Books
Suite 1 SJO 981
P.O. Box 025216
Miami, FL33102
U.S. Fax: 619-4216002
Or Fax: 011-506-232-5613

Please complete and mail to the above address. Use seperate paper if necessary.

l. Have you driven the Pan-American Highway?
   When ?

2. If so, what cities and countries ?

3. Did you find this guidebook helpful ?

4. What are your suggestions for improvement?

5. What changes did you find in required documents?

6. What were the principal cities on your route?

7. What were the road conditions?

8. What dates did you drive this route?

9. Dld you use (_) hotels (_) motels (_) Other

10. What hotels and motels did you use?

11. How did prices compare with this book?

12. How were the service and accomodations?

13. What were your costs at each border?

14. May we use your name if we decide to tell about your experiences to help others in the future?

(_____) Yes   (_____) No   Please Initial:_____

15. You may write an outline or story of your trip and experiences if you wish. We will contact you if we decide to use your material in the next edition of this guide.

Thank You.

Optional: (Please Print)

Your Name: _____

Street: _____

City: _____

State: _____ Zip: _____

SUGGESTED READING

MEXICO

RV Travel in Mexico, by John Howels. Gateway Books, Oakland, CA.

The Peoples Guide to Mexico, by Carl Franz. John Muir Publications, P.O. Box 613, Sante Fe, NM 87504. The best book ever written on the subject. It has been around for over twenty years.

Mexico. Lonley Planet Publications, 155 Filbert Street, Suite 251, Oakland CA 94607.

MexicoTravel Book 1996, by AAA. American Automoblie Association, 1000 AAA Drive, Heathrow, FL 32746.

Mexico and Central America Handbook. Passport Books, 4255 West Toulty Ave., Lincolnwood, Il. 60646.

Mexico Handbook. Moon Publications, Inc., P.O. Box 3040. Chico CA 95927.

CENTRAL AMERICA

Central America Guide, by Paul Glassman. Open Road Publishing, P.O. Box 20226, Columbus Circle Station, New York, NY 10023.

Central America On a Shoestring. Lonley Planet, 155 Filbert Street, Suite 251, Oakland, Ca 94607.

Central America, by Berkreley Guides. Fodor Travel Publications, 201 E 50th Street, New York, NY 10022.

Frommer's Guide to Costa Rica, Guatemala and Belize on $35 a Day. Prentice Hall Press.

Travellers Central American Survival Kit, by Simon Calder. Vacation Works Publications, 9 Park End Street, Oxford OX1 1HJ, England.

BELIZE

The New Key to Belize, by Stacy Ritz. Ulysses Press, 3286 Adeline Street, Suite 1, Berkeley, CA 94703.

Belize Retirement Guide, by Bill and Claire Gray. Preview Publishing, 18627 Brookhurst Street, Fountain Valley, CA 92708. Tel: (714) 775-0535 FAX: (714) 531-7162.

Adventures in Belize, by Eric Hoffman. Sierra Club, 730 Polk Street, San Francisco, CA 94109.

Belize Handbook, by Chicki Mallan. Moon Publications, P.O. Box 3040, Chico, CA 95927-3040.

GUATEMALA

The New Key to Guatemala, by Richard Harris. Ulysses Press, 3286 Adeline Street, Suite 1, Berkeley, CA 94703.

Guatemala Guide, by Paul Glassman. Open Road Publishing, P.O. Box 20226, Columbus Circle Station, New York, NY 10023.

Guatemala a Natural Destination, by Richard Mahler. John Muir Publications, P.O. Box 613, Sante Fe, NM 78504.

EL SALVADOR

On Your Own In El Salvador, by Jeff Braver. On Your Own Publications, P.O. Box 5411, Charlottesville, VA 22905.

HONDURAS

Honduras, by Paul Glassman. Open Road Publishing, P.O. Box 20226, Columbus Circle Station, New York, NY 10023.

COSTA RICA

The New Key to Costa Rica, by Beatrice Blake and Ann Becher. Ulysses Press, Berkeley, CA . A must for anyone visiting Costa Rica.

The Costa Rica Traveller, by Ellen Searby. Windham Bay Press, P.O.

Box 1198, Occidental, CA 95465. Another great guidebook and essential reading.

Costa Rica Handbook, by Christopher Baker. Moon Publications, P.O. Box 3040, Chico, CA 95927. An extensive guidebook .

Costa Rica, by Eliot Greenspan. Frommer's, 1633 Broadway, New York, NY 10019. An easy-to-use practical guide.

*The Essential Road Guide for Costa Rica, by Bill Baker. Costa Rica Books.

*The Golden Door to Retirement and Living in Costa Rica, by Christopher Howard. Costa Rica Books, Suite 1 SJO 981, P.O. Box 025216, Miami, FL 33102-5216. The *only* book to read on the subject if your goal is to live, retire or invest in Costa Rica.

*Exploring Costa Rica, The Tico Times Annual Guidebook. Costa Rica Books.

Costa Rica - A Travel Survival Kit. Lonley Planet Publications.

Insight Guide to Costa Rica, by Harvey Haber. Houghton Miflin and Prentice - Hall.

*Legal Guide to Costa Rica, by Rodger Peterson. Costa Rica Books.

*Buying Real Estate in Costa Rica, by Bill Baker. Costa Rica Books. .

*Happy Aging With Costa Rican Women by James Y. Kennedy. Also available from Costa Rica Books.

*Costa Rican Spanish Survival Course. Costa Rica Books. Includes a 90-minute cassette.

PANAMA

The Panama Traveller, by David Dudenhoefer. Windham Bay Press, P.O. Box 1198, Occidental, CA 95465. Available in June of 1996. This publisher also has an excellent guide on Costa Rica.

*** All books with asterisks are available from Costa Rica Books. Please see pages 3 and 4 for more details.

NOTES

NOTES

NOTES

NOTES

NOTES